DON'T LET A SHARK
IN YOUR SWIMMING POOL

CAROLYN A. MIRDO

Cover Illustration By Karen Hall

PUBLISHED BY HIGH PITCHED HUM PUBLISHING
321 15th Street North
Jacksonville Beach, Florida 32250

www.highpitchedhum.net

HIGH PITCHED HUM and the mosquito are trademarks
of High Pitched Hum Publishing.

ISBN: 978-1-934666-58-6

Printed in the United States of America

2009

TABLE OF CONTENTS

Chapter 1. What happened to Our Country? 1

Why was Sub-Prime Created? 2-3

Effect of Sub-Prime Financing. 4-5

Get Pre-Approved. 6

Find a Loan Agent, Not a Loan Shark. 7-8

Choosing a Bank, Savings and

Loan or a Mortgage Broker. 9-10

LendingTree.Com. 11

Chapter 2. Understanding Your FICO. 12

Rating Your FICO Scores. 13

Reasons for Declining Credit. 14

The Credit Report. 15

Reading your Credit Report. 16

Pre-Approval Letter. 17

Chapter 3. Conventional Terms and Guidelines. 18-20

The Purchase Contract. 21-23

Buyers and Sellers Market. 24

Writing the Purchase Contract. 25-27

Chapter 4. Conventional Loan Programs, 1-4 Units. 28-33

Loan Amortization Chart. 34

Loan Pricing. 35

Discount Points. 36-37

Locking in Your Interest Rate. 38

Chapter 5.   Qualifying the Conventional Loan Borrower.   39-40

What is Private Mortgage Insurance?   41

Single Family Residence Verses Condo.   42-43

Qualifying for the Loan.   44

Ratio's.   45-47

Credit History.   48-50

Qualifying Income.   51-54

Funds to Close your Loan.   55

Steps to Avoid.   56

Chapter 6.   Refinancing Your Conventional Loan.   57-58

When Should You Refinance?   59-60

Refinance with a Junior Lien.   61-62

Chapter 7.   Who Is FHA?   65-68

FHA Loan Limits.   69

Determining the FHA Loan Amount.   70

Up Front MIP and MMI Charts.   71-72

Refund of Up-Front MIP.   73

What are Sales Concessions?   74-75

Chapter 8.   FHA Terms and Guidelines.   76-79

FHA Loan Programs.   80-81

How to Calculate New ARM Payment   82

Credit Alert system.   83

FHA Allowable and Non-Allowable
Closing Cost.   84-85

HUD's Local Office Directory.   86-92

Chapter 9.   Qualifying the FHA Loan.   93
              Credit Guidelines.   94
              Qualifying Income.   95-96
              Monthly Liabilities.   97-98
              Funds to Close the FHA Loan.   99
              Qualifying the Tri-Plex or Four Plex.   100-102
              Energy Efficient Homes.   103-104

Chapter 10.   FHA Refinance.   105-107
              FHA Streamline Refinance.   108
              FHA Streamline Refinance
              with or without an Appraisal.   109
              Permissible Streamline Refinance.   110

Chapter 11.   Veterans Administration.   113-114
              The VA Appraiser.   115
              Qualifying the VA Loan.   116-117
              Certificate of Eligibility.   118
              VA Entitlement of the Veteran.   119-122
              Restoration of VA Entitlement.   123
              VA Funding Fee.   124-125
              Credit Alert.   126
              Occupancy Requirement.   127-128

Chapter 12   VA Term and Guidelines.   129-132
              Qualifying the VA Loan.   133
              Qualifying Income.   134-136
              Debt from Credit Report.   137-138
              List of Compensating Factors.   139
              Child Care Statement.   140

	Maintenance / Utilities.	141
	What is Residual Income?	142-143
	What is a VA Sales Concession?	144-145
	VA Allowable Closing Cost.	146
	VA Closing Cost the Veteran Cannot Pay.	147
	VA Regional Offices.	148-149
Chapter 13.	VA Refinance.	150
	Veterans with Sub-Prime Loans.	151
	VA Interest Rate Reduction Refinance (IRRRL).	152
	Refinancing VA Rental Property.	153
Chapter 14.	Loan Assumptions.	156
	How to Assume an Existing Mortgage.	157
	Examples of a Land Contract.	158
	Examples of a Loan Assumption.	159-160
	Typical Loan Assumption Contract.	161
	Compare Assumption to New Loan Origination.	162
Chapter 15.	Subordinate Financing.	163
	Seller Carry back Second Mortgage.	164
	Discounted Mortgage Notes.	165
	The Seller's Protection.	166
Chapter 16.	Foreclosures in Today's World.	167
	Non Profit Loan Counseling Loan Modification.	168
	Buying A Foreclosure.	169-170
	Good-By.	171-172

INTRODUCTION

As the world turns upside down, and I sit in my over 55 community in St. Augustine, Florida, with my blood boiling, I wrote "Don't Let a Shark in Your Swimming Pool."

What has happened to our Country has prompted me to write this book. The mortgage industry has destroyed peoples' lives by greed. I am just one person, but I want to do my part to see that never happens again.

My name is Carolyn Mirdo. As a retired loan underwriter from JPMorgan Chase and a former banking officer from the mortgage banking industry with over twenty-five years in mortgage banking and five years in real estate sales. My qualifications for writing this book are as follows: I was a senior loan underwriter for major banks and saving and loan lending institutions in southern California and Florida. As an officer, I wrote training manuals and taught government loan programs to loan processors and loan agents. My experience includes all aspects of pre and post loan closing as well as working as a field loan agent in both wholesale and retail mortgage lending.

I set up the FHA department for two lenders in Irvine, California and brought the mortgage companies through their HUD Test Cases for FHA Stamp Approval. Once test cases are approved, this process enables the mortgage company to originate FHA loans. Any Direct Endorsement Underwriter who has set up a government department for a mortgage company can tell you, the process is grueling. HUD is very demanding and rightfully so, after all, HUD will be putting their trust in that mortgage company to deliver credible loan packages.

All mortgage finance books in the marketplace today are written by either real estate attorneys or loan agents. Correct me if I am wrong, but it was the unethical loan agents who got us into this mess. It is the underwriter, not the loan agent, that makes the decision if a loan is approved or denied. This book is written from an underwriter's point of view.

This book is a must read for those of you wanting to buy a home. The book will help you determine what loan program is best for you, Conventional, FHA or VA. You will be able to determine if it is in your best interest to pay Discount Points, as well as know the difference between Reasonable Closing Cost and Unreasonable Closing Cost. The book teaches you about Par Pricing, Rebate Pricing and Loan Locks. You will learn about and explore Loan Assumptions, Subordinate Financing, Foreclosures and more. There are many examples and scenarios written for easy understanding.

I do not intend to shed a negative light on loan agents in general, on the contrary, there are many wonderful loan agents who really take their work seriously and would never put their clients in a dangerous position. Those agents will probably recommend my book. My intention is meant to help you weed out the good agent from the Shark.

Sincerely,

Carolyn A. Mirdo

ACKNOWLEDGMENT

There are so many people I want to thank for helping me put together this body of work. Like they say, it does take a village. I want to thank my editor, Jerry Livingston of Hanks Livingston in Jacksonville, Florida for his patience and encouraging me to go forward with this project. He felt like I do, the material needs to be available in the marketplace.

I had a vision for the cover of my book but it took the brilliant artistic talent of Karen Hall to bring that vision to life. Karen is a free lance artist and a retired art teacher from Kansas City, Kansas.

I want to thank the wonderful men and woman that work for FHA and VA. I am sorry if I made a pest of myself, but they went beyond the call of duty to assist me with answering my questions because of guideline changes.

Last but not least, I want to thank my beloved granddaughter Alexandra Ezcurra and my son-in-law Dr. John Ezcurra for all their hard work on the computer and their perseverance giving me computer instruction. I could have never finished this book without them.

CHAPTER 1

WHAT HAPPENED TO OUR COUNTRY?

Our country has experienced the largest bailout of the banks and Wall Street in American history, all of it a direct result of the mortgage banking industry meltdown. Right or wrong, only time will tell if it was a necessary action. Then not long after the bailout, the big three American automobile factories wanted a bailout, also. Where will the insanity end?

What has happened to people wanting to buy a home in the last five or six years is criminal. The sub-prime loan industry brought this nation to its knees. Now, we the taxpayers are all paying the price.

There are loan sharks out there. My hope is to give you some insight so you may recognize the shark when you meet one, and you certainly do not need a "shark in your swimming pool." Please, don't get me wrong, there are many wonderful hardworking loan agents. You just have to be sure your agent has your best interest at heart, and not his or her own pocketbook. If a loan agent is truly caring about their clients and puts their clients interest first, referrals will come, and with that comes success.

I was going to leave this chapter out of the book because of its sensitive nature, but I remember like it was yesterday, something that happened almost 20 years ago. I walked into a loan agent's office and there he was, bigger than life with a razor blade in his hand, I kid you not. You might be wondering what was he doing with a razor blade? He was falsifying someone's paycheck stub.

With the technology we have today it is very easy to alter qualifying exhibits. I have caught loan agents falsifying tax returns, bank statements and other exhibits, and that is not the loan agent you want. Sure you love the house, you can see yourself living in that house, it is your dream home. Trust me, if you cannot afford the home without the help of an unethical loan agent, you do not want that home in your life. You will grow to hate that house because it will become a hardship and your life will become a living hell.

A good loan agent will not try to place you in a mortgage loan you cannot afford. Only a shark would do that. A good loan agent will guide you if you are buying a home you cannot afford, and will display a fiduciary relationship with you.

Sub-prime loan programs brought out the worst in some loan agents. Sub-prime is a higher interest rate loan because of the borrower's poor credit and low credit scores. Sub-prime is a loan program that a borrower is placed in when the borrower's credit does not meet investor guidelines, such as Fannie Mae, Freddie Mac or Ginnie Mae. Sub-prime otherwise called B-C paper, has been around a long time but it has not been used to that extent. Please, NEVER accept a sub-prime loan. If you do not qualify for conventional, FHA or VA loan programs, then wait until you do.

Why was sub-prime created? Before going down that road, look back to what got us in this mess. In the 1960's, mortgage lenders were known to redline areas. They would not make a mortgage loan in poor areas of town.

Not that many years ago, a moral outrage rang out in the media's ear, "Minorities cannot get the same mortgage loans that white people get." Banks were accused of not approving mortgage loan applications for minorities as often as they did for white people. All of this was an opening salvo in a campaign to get Congress to pass laws forcing lenders to loan money to people they otherwise would not lend money to.

By 2000, reverse red-lining was under way. Lenders were going after the poor and most vulnerable people. They offered no money down financing, and no income verification. They created the Liar Loan. Some loan agents could care less when putting a home buyer in a loan the buyer could not afford. The agent just cared about making money. Loan approval or denial had nothing to do with it, if you were a minority. I have never met an underwriter who would base a decision on race. This was pure propaganda by the media. Among the many reasons an underwriter would deny a loan application are poor credit, credit does not meet investor guidelines, insufficient income, insufficient funds to close the loan, unverifiable information, unacceptable collateral, unacceptable work history, bankruptcy or foreclosure.

It is a shame what happened to so many people. And believe me, there were many people who were put into dangerous mortgage loans who did not belong there.

I would bet a dime to a dollar that at least half of all the people who were given a sub-prime loan, qualified for an FHA loan program. But, for one reason or another, they were never offered an FHA loan.

FHA is "A" paper pricing. The loan agent stood to make much more money if the borrower was placed in a sub-prime loan program. Now, I say that is criminal, wouldn't you?

What you need to understand is that, in the mortgage banking industry there is what is called "A" paper and "B - C" paper.

"A" paper, would be a conventional loan program, conforming and jumbo loans as well as government loan programs, such as FHA and VA loans. These loans would get you the best interest rates in the marketplace. "B - C" paper, otherwise called sub-prime loan programs, are for more risky borrowers and are more expensive with higher interest rates, and the terms of the loans are not favorable to the borrower.

Let us look at an example of what happened to many people who qualified for

FHA financing but were never offered FHA because the loan agent stood to make a larger commission by selling the borrower a sub-prime loan, or maybe the agent was not an approved FHA lender. I will illustrate the two loan programs, FHA and sub-prime and show the effect on the borrower down the road.

Example:

Imagine Miss Minnie has a credit score of 609. She is buying a home for a sale price of $110,000. She would not qualify for a conventional loan because her credit score is below 680, but she would qualify for an FHA loan which is also "A" paper pricing and require a 3% down payment at the time.

FHA is a lot more forgiving on derogatory credit if a good explanation letter is provided to the lender. FHA does require up-front mortgage insurance premium, otherwise called (MIP) on all new loans. Up front mortgage insurance is what helps keep FHA solvent, this is explained in detail in the FHA Chapters.

Miss Minnie wanted to close her home loan before the end of the year, which in this case was 2003. The example illustrates principal and interest payments only and guidelines for that time period.

FHA: Interest rate @ 5.75%   30-year fixed rate:

Sales price of home	$110,000.00	
3% Down payment	- 3,300.00	
Base loan amount	$106,700.00	
Up-Front MIP 2.25%	2,400.00	
Total loan amount	$109,100.00	Monthly Payment = $636.05

Let us use the same scenario with conventional sub-prime financing and a required 5.0% down payment. 30-year adjustable rate mortgage (Arm), due in five years. This program is called a 5/30 ARM interest only.

Interest only @ 7.50% fixed for 5 years. At the 5 year term, the loan will roll to an adjustable rate loan, but the loan has 5 % cap. So the rate could increase to 12.5%.

Sales price of home	$110,000.00	
Down payment of 5%	-5,500.00	
	_____	
Total loan amount	$104,500.00	Monthly payment = $653.13

Worse case scenario:	Present mortgage payment.	$653.13
	Maturity rollover 12/2008	12.50% interest
	New payment after 12/2008	$1,115.02

Is it any wonder the people who opted for the sub-prime loan felt trapped? Keep in mind that nothing was paid on the principal in five years, and Miss Minnie still owes $104,500. The principal payment that should have been paid each month for those five years will now become due or it will be added to the new payment structure. Shame on her loan agent. Miss Minnie should have been offered an FHA loan.

I will take you through conventional loan programs such as conforming and jumbo loans, as well as government loan programs such as FHA and VA. Conforming loans are loans the lenders sell to Fannie Mae and Freddie Mac.

Government loans are sold to Ginnie Mae. Conventional and government loans vary with the market place.

After reading this book, you will have the tools you need to determine what loan program will be best for you. Maybe, I can also help give you a sense of how to screen a good agent from the sharks that give the industry a bad name. You will realize when it is in your best interest to pay discount points. You will be shown the difference between "reasonable" closing cost and "unreasonable" closing cost. Your loan agent is the person who will give you a pre-approval letter to purchase your home. Your pre-approval letter is really based on your credit report, your credit score, and the verbal information you give your loan agent. The agent will give you a list of items to start the loan process. Such items as two years of W-2s, current paycheck stubs, bank statements and maybe tax returns, depending on the field of work you are in. These items will be needed to back up the information you provided, so please, be accurate. The agent can not start the process without your exhibits.

A lot of people forget about loan assumptions. We will explore the possibility of assuming an existing loan and save thousands of dollars in closing costs.

Get Pre-Approved

Pre-approval is exactly that, it is not a final loan approval. Your loan does not get final loan approval until the last hour. Once you bring your loan agent the exhibits requested, your loan will be assigned a loan processor. Believe me, good loan processors are worth their weight in gold. They can make or break your loan. After your loan is completely processed, it is then sent to the underwriting department for final loan approval. A good loan processor will recognize a problem up front and contact the underwriting department for guidance to resolve the problem.

The processor destroyed my own loan, believe it or not. While building the home we presently own, the processor ordered the appraisal too soon. I sent her a copy of my purchase contract and a copy of upgrades from the design center. On the appraiser order sheet, the processor entered the sales price from the purchase contract but did not add the design center upgrades to the purchase price, which is customary with new construction. That was a $21,000 difference. As a result, the appraised value came in $21,000 too low. The lender would not order a new appraisal or return my appraisal fee for the mistake. The funny part about this, is that the lender was my employer. Needless to say, I took my loan elsewhere.

Finding A Loan Agent

A recommendation by a family member or a friend is always the best, but sometimes there are no recommendations, and is not always wise to get a recommendation from your real estate agent. Have you heard of kickbacks? Some real estate agents would never accept kickbacks, but others demand them.

I would interview a minimum of three loan agents before making a decision on who will earn my loan. You should look for the experience of the loan agent, and how long the agent has been in the mortgage industry, that is not to say a new loan agent cannot be a good agent, as long as he has a benefactor. Look for the integrity of that agent. After conversing, you can usually sense the quality of a person. Can the company perform all loan programs, government loans as well as conventional? A lender needs to be approved by FHA and VA to originate government loans. Also, compare the interest rates and the closing cost of each lender because they can vary considerably.

With each interview, bring your credit report with you. Ask the loan agent to see their programs and the best rates they can offer you. Ask them to give you a "Good Faith Estimate." DO NOT let the lender run your credit report. Each time your credit report is run, it lowers your credit score. When you choose your lender, at that time and only at that time, should you let the lender run your credit report.

Questions To Ask Your Loan Agent

Here are some questions to keep in mind when seeking a loan agent. This person will be your representative during your home loan process, so choose carefully.

- How long has the agent been originating loans?

- Will you be charged a relock fee if your rate expires? If you are locked in to a rate and the rate drops will you get the lower rate? (Most lender will negotiate.)

- Will the agent show you a rate sheet? If there is hesitation, run as fast as you can.

- What will the commission be on your loan? A fair commission is 1 % -1.50% of the loan amount. Some will say they do not charge a commission, the loan shows a 1% loan origination fee, in reality this is their commission.

- Rebate pricing means higher interest to you for cash back at closing. Ask the agent if you choose rebate pricing will the rebate pass to you and not the lender.

- Can this company originate government loans as well as conventional?

- What other loans has the agent closed from both private parties and real estate agents. Ask for references.

CHOOSING A BANK,

SAVINGS & LOAN, OR MORTGAGE BROKER

Mortgage Brokerage House: Is a non-supervised lender, they are under the umbrella of a supervised lender. A mortgage broker has a full menu of interest rates and programs. A brokerage house is approved by many wholesale lenders who are the banks and savings & loans. The broker will get rate sheets faxed over each morning around 11a.m. The rate sheets from the wholesale lenders will reflect the programs offered and the interest rates for that day. The broker could be approved by 10 or 12 wholesale lenders, so you will have a wide variety of rates to choose from. On the other hand a brokerage firm usually has higher closing cost fees. They are not regulated in the same manner as a bank or savings & loan.

Banks and Savings & Loans: Are supervised lending institutions and they have guidelines they must follow even though they were deregulated in 1999. As for interest rates, a bank only has it's own product to sell. One day a banks interest rates might be high, the next day low. A bank usually has lower closing cost fees than a mortgage broker, who actually is the middle man.

After reviewing the, "Good Faith Estimate" from three or more lenders, you will be able to see where you can find the most bang for your buck. Evaluate the fees and the interest rates. That way you can make a decision that is right for you.

In closing a home loan, there are two kind of fees. They are "Recurring fees" and "Non-Recurring fees." The recurring fees are the property tax, homeowner's insurance and the per-diem interest on your home loan. They are called recurring fees because they must be paid every year. The figures will change depending on the time of month you close your loan.

The fees you should be concerned with are the non-recurring fees. These fees are one time closing cost fees to close your loan. The non-recurring fees will not change. Some lenders have high non-recurring fees, what I mean by that, is they tend to nickel and dime you to death with frivolous fees such as a fax fee, a warehouse fee, a courier fee, etc. Get your fees up front on your "Good Faith Estimate" so there are no surprises at closing. If you find frivolous fees, ask your loan agent to have them waived.

LENDINGTREE.COM

LendingTree.com is quite the trend right now. Just go on your computer and you will get three offers from lenders. My only objection to using the computer for your home loan, is that you will never have a face to face interview with your loan agent. Mind you, I do not want to shed a negative light on LendingTree in any way. My daughter used LendingTree and had a very successful experience. I just think there is something to be said for having a personal relationship with your loan agent.

When you apply with LendingTree, you will get three offers from three different lending institutions such as banks, savings and loans and mortgage brokerage houses. Everything is done on the computer except for the actual closing of your loan.

Just keep one thing in mind. The lowest interest rate may not always be the best. Look at the interest rate, the closing cost, and the service of a company. Can the company go the extra mile for you if needed at closing? Does the loan agent sit behind a desk or computer all day or does the agent actually go out into the field when something needs to be hand delivered so you can close your loan on time? It is like getting three estimates to repair your car. You should also consider the company that offers great customer service and has a reputation for it.

CHAPTER 2

UNDERSTANDING YOUR FICO

FICO SCORES: Your mortgage loan approval will depend heavily on the FICO scoring system. FICO stands for Fair Isaac Corporation. It is used by the top three credit reporting bureaus in the United States. A Tri-Merge credit report involves pulling your credit from all three credit reporting agencies:

EXPERIAN	TRANS UNION	EQUIFAX
1-888-397-3742	1-800-888-4213	1-800-685-1111

The lender will establish your FICO score, which in turn will determine the interest rate you will be charged for your home loan. Each agency will report a credit score. To determine your FICO score, the lender will throw out the high credit score and the low credit score, and your middle score will become your FICO score. The same is done for your spouse, but with a spouse on the loan, or any other second party, the lower of the two middle scores will become your joint FICO score.

For example:

| Mickey's three scores: | 682, 720, 702 | Mickey's middle score: 702 |
| Minnie's three scores: | 703, 721, 710 | Minnie's middle score: 710 |

The lower of the borrowers combined middle scores is 702. The loan FICO score is 702.

FICO scores are rated as follows:

340 - 619	POOR	620 - 659	FAIR
660 - 749	GOOD	750 - 840	EXCELLENT

The lower the FICO score, the higher the interest rate. That is just the way it is.

If your FICO score is low and you do not qualify for "A" paper price, I would suggest you wait six months and try again. Take all the necessary steps to clean up your credit. If you pay off credit cards, do not close the accounts. Closing the accounts will only bring your FICO score down further. It is better to leave the cards alone in a drawer with a zero balance. Be diligent about paying your bills on time. Never take out a loan where payments are deferred. Furniture stores, computer stores and home improvement stores are notorious for offering this type of credit. They only create a negative effect on your credit report.

The best way I have found to monitor your score effectively is through the score watch program "myFICO.com." The nice part about this service is that, if anything derogatory appears on your credit report, you can dispute it in a timely manner.

There Are Many Reasons For Declining Credit Scores:

- Balances on revolving accounts being more than 50 percent of the credit-limit

- Too many inquiries on your credit report

- Reporting of late payments, (counts for about 35 percent of your credit score)

- Heavy credit users

- A public judgement, tax lien, and even unpaid parking tickets

- Collections and charge-offs

- Bankruptcy / Foreclosure

- Financing companies lower your score more than using banks or department stores.

Correcting An Error On Your Credit Report:

Even credit reporting agencies make mistakes. Contact the agency that reported the error and you will probably be directed to the company that reported the late payment. Contact that company and iron out the problem. Once the problem has been cleared, ask the company for a signed letter on it's letterhead stating that the error has been cleared. Even if the credit reporting company cannot clear the item from your credit report in a timely manner, don't let that hold you up from making a loan application, the letter from the company will suffice and you should have no problem obtaining your loan.

Credit Report

Probably the first step to home ownership is to pull your credit report. You can order your credit report by using your computer. You are entitled to one free credit report a year. If you are buying a home with your spouse, you will need a credit report for both of you. There are companies that advertise " Free Credit Report", but they actually charge $39.95 for each report.

The only free credit report is from "Annual Credit Report.com". The company offers a free credit report once a year from the three credit reporting agencies. This site will ask if you want a tri-merge credit report at a fee of $7.95. I would recommend you spring for the $7.95 because you will need all three reporting agencies to determine your credit scores for your home loan. The credit reporting agencies are Experian, Trans Union and Equifax as noted earlier in this chapter.

Print two copies, one for your files and bring the other to take with you while you are interviewing lenders. Do Not let the lenders pull your credit report until you decide which lender will handle your loan. The lender can look at your credit report that you bring into the office and give you an interest rate and loan program from that credit report. Each and every time your credit report is pulled, it lowers your credit score. Some loan agents will tell you, that is not true, but don't you believe it. It is absolutely true.

Reading Your Credit Report:

In reading your credit report, go over the accounts shown to be sure they are accurate. If you find something that does not belong to you, call the credit reporting agency that is reporting the account. You might have a common name, or if you are a Junior, it is not uncommon to have your father's account show up on your credit report.

First Column: Reflects the creditor along with the account number.

Second Column: The date the account was opened and right below the date will be the last payment that was received by the creditor.

Third Column: The opening dollar amount borrowed when the account was opened and right below that number is the current outstanding balance.

Fourth Column: The term of the loan, either a mortgage, installment or revolving account, and below the identification will be the monthly payment due.

Fifth Column: MOP will reflect what type of loan.

Sixth Column: Your payment history, 30-60-90. Zeros are good, and zeros would mean no late payments.

Seventh Column: The word "TYPE" is telling you what borrower the account belongs to. I-B means the first borrower on the loan application and I-C stands for co-borrower, so the debt that shows I-C would belong to the second borrower on the loan application.

Pre-Approval Letter

When you choose a lender for your home loan, you can then give permission to the agent to order your credit report. The loan agent, in turn, will give you a pre-approval letter to take to your real estate agent. You will have a lot more clout with getting your purchase contract offer accepted if you have a pre-approval letter from your loan agent.

It is very important, that once you have a pre-approval letter from your loan agent you do not make any large purchases, such as, buying a car or furniture without talking to your loan agent first. It may not affect your loan if you are a strong borrower. But you might be a marginal borrower and you want to be sure you are not jeopardizing the purchase of your new home.

Once your loan processor orders your tri-merge credit report, the report has a 90 day life before it expires. Actually, that means, 90 days to underwriting and 120 days to closing your loan. It is a very sad day for everyone when a credit report expires and has to be updated. Now, guess what? If the updated credit report reflects a new car loan, or other large purchases the borrower may no longer qualify for the home loan. Don't let that happen to you.

CHAPTER 3

BASIC CONVENTIONAL TERMS AND GUIDELINES

- **AMORTIZATION:** The liquidation of a financial obligation on an installment basis; also recovery, over a period, of cost or value.

- **APPRAISAL:** Required by a lender to determine property value. The appraiser must be licensed by the state and be an approved appraiser on the lender's panel.

- **ASSUMPTION OF MORTGAGE:** A transfer or taking over, of an existing mortgage loan from the seller of the property. The purchaser executes an assumption agreement signed by all parties.

- **CERTIFICATE OF OCCUPANCY:** Required on new construction as evidence, that the county has inspected the property, and construction is complete and done in a workman like manner and meets construction code.

- **CHATTEL MORTGAGE:** A mortgage on personal property. A mobile home is considered chattel property, it is not considered real property.

- **CONDOMINIUM (Condo):** A system of individual fee ownership of units in a multifamily structure, combined with joint ownership of common areas of the structure and the land.

- **ESCROW / IMPOUND ACCOUNT:** An account set up by the lender to collect your property taxes, homeowners insurance and flood insurance. In mortgage states, the account is called an escrow account and in trust deed states, the account is called an impound account.

- **HOMEOWNERS ASSOCIATION (HOA):** A homeowners association is independent and governs the Declaration of Covenants, Conditions, Restrictions, the homeowners association by-laws and the association budget.

- **INDEX:** The index is the measure used in adjustable mortgages at the time of adjustment. It is usually based on the T-Bill or the 11th District Cost of Funds index.

- **LOAN TO VALUE (LTV):** Your loan amount will be based on the sales price of the home or the appraised value of the home, with the lessor of the two divided into your loan amount.

- **MARGIN:** The margin is the spread stated on the adjustable rate rider to the note.

- **MORTGAGE:** A mortgage is a written contract whereby specific property is hypothecated to create a debt or obligation in parts of the country, (mostly east coast and mid-west) to guarantee your loan. "Hypothecate" means to make property security for a loan without delivering possession of the property to the lender.

- **PLANNED UNIT DEVELOPMENT (PUD):** A PUD could refer to attached or detached housing. It is different from a condo because you own the land the property sits on. In a condo you own air space, as a percentage of the entire complex.

- **PRINCIPAL, INTEREST, TAXES AND INSURANCE (PITI):** Monthly house payment of Principal, Interest, Property Taxes, Homeowners Insurance and Flood Insurance (if applicable).

- **PRINCIPAL AND INTEREST (P&I):** Monthly house payment of principal & interest payments, not including property taxes and homeowners insurance held in the escrow account. Loans of 80% LTV or less, are not required to have an escrow account.

- **PRIVATE MORTGAGE INSURANCE (PMI):** Private mortgage insurance is required if your down payment on the subject property is less than 20% of the purchase price or appraised value, the lessor of the two.

- **SINGLE FAMILY RESIDENCE (SFR):** One unit, could be a single family detached home, condo or a Pud. In a condo or a Pud, homeowners association dues are included in the ratios. These dues are not collected through the escrow account, and you will be billed directly.

- **SUBORDINATION CLAUSE:** Clause in a second or junior lien permitting retention of priority for prior liens. May also be used in a first or senior lien permitting it to be subordinated to a subsequent lien, such as a construction loan.

- **TRUST DEED:** This is the instrument which transfers (conveys) to bare legal title of a property to a trustee to be held pending fulfillment of an obligation, usually the repayment of a loan to a beneficiary. Trust Deed states are mostly in the western part of our country. Escrow officers are used to close the loan in a trust deed state, unlike a mortgage state, real estate attorneys are used to close the loan.

- **UNITS:** Two to four units are a duplex, three units or four units. Anything beyond four units is underwritten in the commercial loan department and is considered a major loan.

Signing The Purchase Contract

Before signing the bottom line of a purchase contract, be sure to read this entire chapter. I want to make you aware of a few points. My objective is loan financing, not real estate sales, but in some respects they do go hand and hand. Whether you are using a professional real estate agent to navigate you through the process or you are buying your home directly from the seller of the property, it could be costly if you don't protect yourself.

I want to cover several very important points that should be included in the contract to protect your earnest money deposit, keeping in mind that every state has its own real estate laws and ethics laws.

In the state of Georgia, for instance, the state does not require builders to have a builder's license. I know that's very hard to believe. California, on the other hand, does an overkill with ethics laws. Alabama is probably one of the worst states regarding ethics, their theory is "Buyer Beware."

The example I am about to share with you actually happened to my daughter and son-in-law when they bought their home in Birmingham, Alabama.

They had narrowed in on a new gate-guarded subdivision with a beautiful recreation center. The center included swimming pools, tennis courts with lessons, and more. They were told that when one buys in that subdivision, the amenities center is included in the price of the home. That, in itself, should have set off a red flag.

Once my daughter and her family moved into their new home, they tried to use the recreational center, only to find out that the entry fee was $2,000 to join, plus monthly dues if you decide to join. This fact had never been disclosed. My daughter called an attorney and he said Alabama law does not protect the public.

He said the law actually read, "Buyer Beware." In my daughter's case, her agent assumed the recreational center was included with ownership since the listing in MLS did not reflect otherwise. She was kind enough to contribute $1,000 toward the $2,000 entry fee. The buyer's agent felt the seller's agent should contribute the other $1,000, since the seller's agent did not disclose the fee in the listing agreement. Needless to say, my daughter is still waiting.

If you are buying a home directly from the seller without the benefit of a real estate agent, always have a real estate attorney look over your contract. It is well worth the extra $300-$400 for your peace of mind. When writing the contract be sure to insert "Subject to Attorney Approval" within a specified time period agreed to by both parties.

In using a real estate agent, be sure to hire a buyer's agent who will represent you and is looking out for your best interest. Never use the listing agent of the home you want to buy. The listing agent's fiduciary relationship is with the seller, and the agent is under contract with the seller to get the best price for the property. Sometimes people think they will get a better price by using the listing agent because the agent will be earning a commission on both ends of the transaction. I can see how one would think you would be able to negotiate a better price for the property by using the listing agent, but I have not seen it happen since I moved back east.

When I moved to Florida, I was new to the area, but I knew the subdivision where I wanted to buy a home. A new listing went on the market and I called the listing agent for information. She asked if I would like to see the property. We made an appointment to preview the property and my husband and I made an offer to purchase. After going back and forth with a counteroffer twice, I decided not to buy the property, we were $1,200 apart. I guess what really angered me was the agent, because she stood to double-end that transaction. What I mean by that is, the listing agents office would take the 3% commission for the listing, and a 3% commission for the sale. The listing agent could have made that transaction happen, and make twice the commission, but she chose not to. Instead, the property was sold by another real estate office. Now, the listing agent's office commission was 3% instead of 6% commission. You do the numbers. The home was listed for $240,000.

I sold real estate in Southern California from 1976-1982. Those were very hard years. Each and every listing I took for a seller, I would enter into the listing contract that if I sold the property myself, I would adjust the commission from 6% to 4%. Dropping the commission would allow the seller to take a lower offering price for the property. Those times were very much like we have experienced in 2008 and 2009, except back then, the interest rates were rising daily and it became harder to sell property.

A real estate commission has been 6% as far back as I can remember. I know it was 6% in the early sixties because I bought my first home in 1963 with a sales price of $17,500. At the present time, home prices have gone up 10-fold, and in some areas of the country, the average price home is $500,000 or more. If anything, the real estate commission should have been adjusted backward.

Buyers Market / Sellers Market

First know what the market is before making an offer to purchase a home. At the present time, we are in a buyers market with our country in a recession and home sales at an all time low. A seller's market would be a hot real estate market, when property moves quickly and sellers get asking price or higher for their property. In a seller's market there are bidding wars, and the seller is not motivated to give sales concessions to a buyer to sell their home. The opposite happens in a buyer's market, the seller is very motivated to work with a buyer to make a sale happen.

In negotiating a contract, there are two thought processes you should consider. Of course, everyone wants a property for the best possible price. That is human nature, but let us look at another angle. The seller has a bottom line to net from the property being sold, and usually the seller does not care how the net dollar amount is obtained.

Instead of concentrating on a lower price, think about offering the seller a higher price, closer to the asking price. In the contract, ask the seller to pay for all or a portion of the non-recurring closing cost and /or a carpet or decorating allowance. You can structure this anyway you like.

If you are buying a condo, maybe you can ask the seller to pay your non-recurring closing cost and also pay one year of the homeowner association dues that are associated with the condo purchase.

In structuring your contract in this manner, you may free up thousands of dollars. Say you ask the seller to pay $3,500 of the non-recurring closing cost and a $4,000 flooring allowance. In turn, you will be adding $7,500 to your loan amount. If your interest rate is 5.75% @ 30 years fixed rate, you will be adding $43.80 to your monthly mortgage payment. If your actual non-recurring closing cost is $5,000, at the closing table you will only be charged $1,500 since the seller is paying $3,500 of your closing cost. You will also be credited $4,000 for flooring, with that amount held in escrow.

Writing The Purchase Contract:

If you are in the process of buying a home, you should be aware of options in writing the purchase contract. You will want to be sure your earnest money deposit is not jeopardized and will be returned to you if the transaction does not materialize. Of course, if you arbitrarily change your mind in the middle of the transaction and the seller's house was taken off the market for a time period, you could lose your earnest money deposit.

There are fewer financial hardships worse than having two house payments. If your home is not sold, be sure to enter the following verbiage into your contract.

- **Contingent upon the successful closing or concurrent closing of 123 Any Street.**

If for any unforeseen reason the property at 123 Any Street does not close, you are protected. You are not bound to complete the purchase of the home and your earnest money deposit will not be forfeited, but will be returned to you.

In the beginning, I mentioned that your Pre-Approval Letter is not final loan approval. Protect yourself by adding the following contingency into the contract:

- **Purchase of 10 Daisy Court is contingent upon final loan approval.**

Anything can happen. You may lose your job or something else might cause your loan to be denied. If you do not get final loan approval, your earnest money deposit will be returned to you if that contingency is in the contract.

APPRAISAL: An Appraisal takes several weeks to complete. When the loan processor begins your loan process, the actual value of the property you are purchasing would not be available at that time. It would be best to arm yourself with adding these words to the contract:

- **10 Daisy Court must appraise for the sales price of $_____ or higher or the sales price will be adjusted.**

Your loan amount is based on the sales price or the appraised value, the lessor of the two.

HOME INSPECTION: A home inspection is imperative in purchasing a home. It is worth every dime. The home inspector is paid by the buyer. Once the inspection is complete, the buyer and seller decide what items are important for immediate repair and what items the buyer can accept. Please don't nickle and dime the seller, especially if the seller is helping with closing cost or other fees.

ROOF INSPECTION: If a roof is 10 years old or older, ask for a roof certification from a licensed roofer so you will know the remaining life of the roof.

SEPTIC TANK: Government loans require a septic tank certification prior to closing the loan. Conventional loans do not have that requirement, but as a homeowner myself, I would recommend that you ask for a certification to ensure the leach lines are clear and the septic tank is in working order.

SWIMMING POOL: You will want the swimming pool inspected by a reliable pool service company. Have the company certify that the pumps are working and the lighting in the pool is by code. If the pool has a heater, that also needs to be inspected. You could ask, in the sales contract that all pool equipment, including the pool sweep, is to be included in the sales price.

CONDOMINIUM OR PLANNED UNIT DEVELOPMENT: As a buyer in such a development, you will want to review the rules and by-laws to make sure you know what you are buying into and that you can live by the rules. Your contract should read:

- **Buyers approval of the Covedients, Conditions, Restrictions (CC&R's) and the Budget and By-Laws.**

PURCHASING A TWO - FOUR UNIT PROPERTY: When buying rental property, you will want to read and approve existing leases the tenants have signed and you will want the tenant's deposit to transfer to the buyer of the property at closing. Make sure it is all spelled out in the purchase contract.

The above are in addition to the standard request of a termite clearance and buyer's approval of a property inspection by an inspector of buyer's choice.

CHAPTER 4

CONVENTIONAL LOANS PROGRAMS
1-4 UNITS

Conforming loan limits vary with times. Effective January 1, 2009 loan limits were raised to $625,000. Any loan above $625,000 is considered a Jumbo loan. One would qualify for a Jumbo loan in the same manner as a conforming loan, the only difference is the lender might require two appraisals from two different appraisers to appraise the property.

A real estate loan department is set up to underwrite one to four unit properties. That would be a single family residence, a duplex, a three unit property or a four unit property. A single family residence could be attached property such as a condo or PUD, or detached property such as a free standing home, modular home or mobile home on it's own lot. Any property larger than four units is underwritten by the commercial loan department. This book covers one to four unit properties only.

Amortized Fixed Rate: The most commonly used conventional loan products are, fixed rate loans with either a 30-year term or a 15-year term. These loans are amortized over the term of the loan for equal payments throughout the loan. Fixed loans are not assumable.

Fixed Rate Balloon: This loan is amortized over 30 years with a balloon payment at the chosen term. Most balloon loans are fixed for three years, five years, seven years or ten years. Once you reach your chosen term, the loan becomes due and payable. That's why it is called a balloon loan. With the balloon loan you have the benefit of a fixed rate until you reach the balloon term. This loan is an excellent loan option if you know that you will be in your home for a short period of time. The fixed rate loan product is not assumable and that includes the balloon loan.

ARM Loans: Adjustable rate mortgages (ARM) are usually tied to the T-bill or the 11th District Cost of Funds Index, otherwise known as Libor. Check both interest rates, (T-bill & Libor) because the savings could be enormous over time. ARM loan programs come with interest rate adjustment changes anywhere from 3 months to 10 years. The Arm loans that are most desirable is the 30/5, 30/7, or the 30/10. These loans, in principal are very much like the balloon loan, except that when you reach your term (30/7 ARM) for example, in seven years, the loan rolls over to an ARM loan. ARM loans are assumable loans.

Figuring New Payment: There are terms you will need to become familiar with if you are considering an ARM loan, such as the index, margin, adjustment cap and life cap. The index is the 30-day rate of the T-bill or 11th District Cost of Funds. The current 30-day index can be found in the business section of your newspaper. The margin varies with different loan programs. You will agree on a margin at the time of loan application and the margin as well as your adjustment cap and life cap will be reflected on your ARM rider to the note.

On average, the margin might be 2.50% to 2.75%. The adjustment cap is the maximum your loan could adjust for each adjustment time period. The average is 2%.

The life cap would be the maximum your loan could adjust for the entire loan term. The life cap is usually 6.00%. I know all of this sounds complicated, but I will give you an example and show you how simple it is to calculate your new payment. All you need to do is add the current index plus the margin and round up to the nearest eighth, for your new interest rate.

Let's say you have a 5% interest rate, 30/5 ARM with a 2% adjustment cap and a 6% life cap. Your margin is 2.75% and the current 30 day T-Bill index is 3.62%

EXAMPLE #1: Index 3.62 + Margin 2.75 = 6.37%. Round up to the nearest 1/8th = new mortgage rate 6.375%. The new rate cannot exceed the 2% adjustment cap. which would have been 7.00%

EXAMPLE #2: Index 4.90 + Margin 2.75 = 7.65%. Round up to the nearest 1/8th = 7.75%. The new rate in this case would be 7.0 % interest, because 7.75% exceeds the 2% cap of the original interest rate of 5.00%.

If you are considering an Adjustable Rate Mortgage, ask your loan agent to prepare a "Worse Case Scenario" worksheet. You will then be able to see, in black and white, how high your mortgage payments could rise.

I would NOT recommend a six-month or one year ARM. Payments increase too fast and you will surely experience payment shock. A better choice would be an ARM loan that is fixed for 5, 7 or 10 years before it adjusts to an adjustable rate for the remaining term of the loan. The fixed/arm program is a safer option.

Negative Amortization Loan: ARM loans are also available as negative amortization loan. Don't be fooled by the low interest rate. The low rate should give you a red flag. If something is too good to be true, it usually is. A negative amortization loan has an interest rate 2%-3% lower than the going market rate. Here is how it works. Each month your payment is not collecting enough interest to cover your loan, so the difference is added to the principal balance you owe on your home. In three or four years, your principal is growing higher and higher because the deferred interest is being tacked on. When you go to sell the property or a balloon payment becomes due, you will be in for the shock of your life. Your principal balance on your home will be thousands of dollars more.

I would NEVER, under any circumstances, recommend a negative amortization loan. Ask your loan agent to be sure your loan is fully amortized with no negative amortization. A lot of people took these loans in areas that were fast growing equity areas, such as California or New York City. Now that the market has dropped, in some cases, people that took these loans owe more on their property than the property is worth.

Graduated Payment Mortgage (GPM): Sometimes called a Buy Down. These loans are popular with the building industry. When market conditions are slow, and builders have a lot of inventory on their hands, the builder may offer to "buy" your interest rate down for a period of time, usually it is a three-year period. Let's say the builder is buying down the rate for three years and the going market interest rate is 6%. The start rate on the GPM loan would be 3% and increase 1% each year. By the fourth year the loan would meet its note rate of 6%. The borrower qualifies for the loan at the note rate not the start rate.

This loan program is not to be confused with a negative amortization loan. In the case of a GPM, the builder pays the difference in the interest rate up-front directly to the lender. You will only find this product available when market conditions are slow, much like we experienced in 2008 and 2009. Builders want to sell their inventory quickly. GPM loans are nice when you can get them. Just be sure you can afford the payment of the note rate when you get to the fourth year. Many people receive a yearly raise that would compensate for the higher payment.

Interest Only: The Interest Only Loan Program is not a bad loan program if you are not concerned with building equity. There is no negative amortization, and your payment is just paying the interest on your loan. Your circumstance, will determine if it would be a good loan program for you, but I would not consider this loan for long term home financing.

One thing to consider, is that when the loan reaches the interest adjustment period, (example 30/5), all principal payments that were deferred for five years will be added to your new payment. Three hundred months will be remaining on the loan, the deferred interest will be spread over the remaining term.

The mortgage industry is going through very turbulent times, lenders are tightening their belts, and are doing away with some programs, and raising their loan to value requirements.

No Doc/Reduced Doc: The program requires very little documentation. This loan program was abused and given to people who would never have qualified for a home loan. In the late 1980's, this loan program was created for the self employed borrower with stellar credit and 25-30% down payment on the property. Lenders had a high comfort level because of the large down payment the borrower made on the property and the borrower's excellent credit. Since that time, the guidelines have become looser and looser. It was mainly this loan program that was abused in the sub prime market. It does not take a genius to realize the catastrophic effect that took place in approving these types of loans for sub prime borrowers.

Prepayment Penalty Clause: When choosing your loan, be sure it does not include a prepayment penalty clause. If you have to sell your home for any reason, such as job transfer, you do not want to be stuck with a penalty for paying off your loan early. Mortgage lenders can charge anywhere from a flat fee too a percentage of the unpaid principal balance of your loan. The penalty for early pay-off can be extremely costly.

LOAN AMORTIZATION CHART

The following table will help you to determine your mortgage payment. Simply multiply the factor by the loan amount you wish to borrow = monthly payment.

Example:

30 year loan @ 5.50% interest; $150,000 loan amount X 5.68 = $852.00

15 year loan @ 5.00% interest; $150,000 loan amount X 7.91 = $1,186.50

Interest Rate	15-year factor	30-year factor
4.00	7.40	4.77
4.50	7.65	5.07
5.00	7.91	5.37
5.50	8.18	5.68
6.00	8.44	6.00
6.50	8.72	6.33
7.00	8.99	6.65
7.50	9.28	7.00
8.00	9.56	7.34
8.50	9.85	7.69
9.00	10.15	8.05
9.50	10.45	8.41
10.00	10.75	8.78
10.50	11.06	9.15
11.00	11.37	9.53
11.50	11.69	9.91
12.00	12.01	10.29

LOAN PRICING AND DISCOUNT POINTS:

Loan pricing might seem very complicated, so I will try to help you gain some knowledge in this area before meeting your loan agent. I hope I can give you an idea of when it would benefit you to pay for rebate pricing over par pricing, and whether you should pay discount points or save your money.

Par Pricing: Par pricing means the current market interest rate, which changes daily and sometimes hourly. With par pricing, you will not have to pay to buy your interest rate down. Your interest rate is reduced when you buy discount points. The higher the points, the lower the interest rate. Par price does not cost you anything.

Premium Pricing: Sometimes this is called "rebate" pricing, because it is exactly that. You pay a higher interest rate and you get a rebate. Why would you want to pay a higher interest rate? The reasons are many, but let us say you do not intend to stay in your home for a long period of time, and you need extra funds for closing costs. That is all well and good, but be careful you are not charged rebate pricing and the loan agent is the one to benefit from the rebate. I have seen it time and again where the agent actually keeps your rebate. You might say, is this legal? It is not only legal, it happens all the time. Don't let it happen to you. This is why you want to see the daily rate sheet, so you can see if you are getting what you paying for.

Rate Sheet Example:

Let us say, the par price is 5.750% interest with zero cost to you. The premium price is 6.00% interest at 0.25% Rebate. If you decided to take 6% interest for your home loan, and your loan amount is $100,000 you would receive $250.00 credit at closing. You want that $250.00 in your pocket, not your loan agents pocket.

Discount Points: Discount points are shown on the rate sheet below par pricing. Discount points lower your interest rate. Should you pay discount points? Everyone likes to get the best interest rate they can, but there are several issues you will need to weigh. If you plan to stay in the property, or keep the property, for a long period of time, it would benefit you to pay discount points. On the other hand, if you know you will be in the property for less than five years or so, and have no intention of keeping the property, then you would be wasting your money in most cases. If your discount points are not financed into your loan, and you paid for the points through the closing, you will be able to take the discount points as a tax deduction. Use the figure from your HUD 1 (closing statement).

DISCOUNT POINTS EXAMPLE:

LOAN AMOUNT $100,000/ 30 YEAR TERM @ 6% Par = $599. Per month P&I

Discount Points:	Interest Rate:
0.125	5.875%
0.250	5.750
0.375	5.625
0.500	5.500
0.625	5.375
0.750	5.250
0.875	5.125
1.000	5.000

Let's say you plan to stay in your home, or at least keep the property and turn it into a rental property until it is paid off in 30 years. You decide to buy your interest rate down to 5% and pay one discount point at a cost of $1,000. This is a very smart move. For your $1,000 investment, your savings over the life of the loan will be $16,920.00

Everyone's situation is different. You will need to run your numbers and see if paying points would benefit you. If there is a chance of a job transfer, I probably would not waste the money. Keep in mind, that you can also ask the seller to contribute toward discount points.

Locking In Your Interest Rate: Once you decide on a rate, your loan agent will lock that rate in to guarantee your interest rate until the closing of your loan. In other words, you are reserving your space. Lenders gather their loans in bulk and sell them on the secondary market. The investors who buy closed loans are Fannie Mae, Freddie Mac, Ginny Mae and other investors such as banks.

If you lock your loan for a 45-day lock, the lender is counting on that loan to close before 45 days to fill its pool commitment to the investor. If your lock is 30 days, the loan must close within 30 days. That is usually why the lender charges a penalty when your loan does not close during the lock time and the lock expires. The lender usually charges a relock fee as a penalty. Ask your loan agent to have the relock fee waived. Again, we get back to market conditions if your request will be honored.

You can lock your rate anywhere from 10 days to 60 days. Anything longer than 60 days would cost too much in the way of the interest rate. The less time on the lock, the better the interest rate and vice versa.

CHAPTER 5

QUALIFYING THE CONVENTIONAL LOAN

Completing The Loan Application, 1003 (TEN-O-THREE)

Your loan agent will likely complete your Loan Application, which is called the 1003. It could be in person or taken over the phone. At some point you will be asked to sign the application. Go over it carefully to be sure all the information the loan agent completed is correct before you sign the bottom line. I can't tell you how often an innocent error was made to the loan application by the loan agent, and caused a problem in the underwriting stage.

It is very important to be veraciously truthful. If you are not, it could come back to bite you. If you feel something will be a problem, talk it over with your loan agent or your loan processor to try to iron out the problem so it won't be a problem in underwriting or worse yet, at closing. Most problems can be solved, believe it or not.

Loan To Value (LTV): The lender places a great deal of emphasis on the property loan to value (LTV). The property is the lender's collateral. The higher the loan to value, the greater the risk for the lender. A loan that is 95% LTV would be a high risk loan for the lender, on the other hand, a 75% LTV would be a comfortable loan for the lender, the reason is simple, the borrower is contributing 25% down payment on the property. Underwriting a very low LTV, such as 30% LTV, I would joke, "this borrower just needs to be breathing for loan approval."

In determining your down payment, take the sales price or the appraised value (the lessor of the two) and times that amount by 80% if you do not want PMI. Lenders want the borrower to have 20% or more down payment into the property. Anything higher than 80% LTV, will require private mortgage insurance.

For Example:

Sales Price:	$110,000.00	Down Payment - $22,000
Appraised Value:	$103,900.00	
Loan Amount:	$ 88,000.00	

$88,000.00 divided by $103,900.00 = 84.7% LTV

I am sure in this case that Mr. Buyer thought he was making a 20% down payment on the purchase of his new home, so private mortgage insurance (PMI) would not be needed. Once the appraisal came in at $103,900, it is a different story. If the seller is not willing to lower the sales price of the home to match the appraised value, the buyer will need to make a decision. Does the buyer still want the home? If the buyer decides to go ahead with the transaction, one of two things will need to happen. The buyer will need to purchase PMI insurance, or the buyer will need to add an additional $4,880.00 to the down payment of the property for an 80% LTV. This example is precisely what I was discussing in the Purchase Contract Section. Be sure to add the verbiage in the purchase contract, "The property is to appraise for the sales price or higher."

What Is Private Mortgage Insurance (PMI)

Conventional loans 80.01% loan to value (LTV) or higher require Private Mortgage Insurance (PMI). This is insurance that will insure against default of the loan. The premium is expensive, and has increased drastically with all the recent foreclosures. The premium is paid monthly with a borrowers mortgage payment directly to the lender. The premium amount is based on risk. You will pay a higher premium for a 95% LTV than you would for an 85% LTV. Not many lenders are offering 95% LTV loans these days as they once did. If you only have a 5% down payment, I would suggest an FHA loan and refer to the FHA section.

To avoid PMI, the lender may offer you a second mortgage, that is a mortgage behind your first mortgage. Many lenders have a program called 80/10/10. The lender will give you a 10% second mortgage with a 10% down payment from you. I would suggest you have your loan agent run the figures both ways to see if the savings is worth having a second mortgage on your home. Remember, the loan agent stands to make a larger commission by selling you a second mortgage.

Why Should I Choose PMI:

One would need to look ahead for the reason a home buyer might choose PMI over a second mortgage. If the property value increases in a hot market and the homeowner can see equity build-up, the homeowner might feel his home is now 80% loan to value or less. In that case, the home owner would order an appraisal and take it to the lender. The lender in turn will remove the PMI from the homeowners loan. If you chose the second mortgage instead of PMI, you would need to keep that loan until it is paid off or refinanced.

Another thought in favor of PMI is that, if the homeowner decided to take out a Home Equity Line Of Credit in the future, the homeowner would be able to do so because the homeowner would not already have a 2nd mortgage on the property.

Single Family Residence Versus Condo

If you are undecided about what type of property you want, whether it is a condo, or a detached single family home. I would suggest you have your loan agent pre-qualify you for a condo, and then qualify you for a single family home without association dues. You might think you can only afford a condo, but because homeowner's association (HOA) dues vary greatly per complex, you might be able to afford a much higher priced home with no homeowner's association dues.

Let us say Mr. Buyer earns $4,800 per month and is considering a condo or a detached house.

Condo: Sales Price; $175,000   Down Payment: 10% = $17,500

Loan Amount: $157,500   @ 6% Interest

P&I	$943.00
Tax	182.00
PMI	79.00
HOA	210.00
Total Housing Expense:	$1,414.00

Take note, that the condo figures do not include the homeowner's property insurance. The property insurance is included in the condo's homeowner's association dues. This is not true for a Pud. The Pud is calculated the same as a single family detached home.

Single Family Residence:

Sales Price: $200,000   Down Payment: 10% = $20,000

Loan Amount: $180,000 @ 6% Interest

Principal & Interest (P&I)	$1,078.00
Property Tax	208.00
Homeowners Property Insurance	75.00
PMI	90.00
Total Housing Expense:	**$ 1,451.00**

In this example, the buyer can afford $25,000 more house in a single family residence. The reason for this? Condo HOA dues are usually substantial. A planned unit development (PUD) is qualified like a single family residence. The property insurance payment is included in the qualifying ratio. The difference between a PUD and a condo is that with a PUD you own your land and with a condo you own airspace or an even percent of the entire complex. The homeowners association dues are usually much less in a PUD, it depends on the development and the amenities they offer.

Qualifying For The Loan

In qualifying a borrower for a home loan, the property tax and homeowner's insurance are included in the ratios. It is impossible to know the property tax rate and insurance rates for different areas throughout the country. Therefore, underwriters use a table that is average for the nation. Some underwriters take the property tax from the appraisal. This practice is fine for resale property only, but is not correct for new construction, since taxes on new construction are paid on raw land, without improvements.

The lenders re-analysis escrow accounts in January each year. What would happen to a borrower when the lender re-analyzes the escrow account the next year? The property tax the following year would be based on the selling price of the home, not raw land. The borrower could be in a home he could not afford and could suffer payment shock when the property taxes re-adjust. This is why underwriters use an average scale for qualifying purposes in figuring the ratios of a home loan. The following are the most common figures used by underwriters. I have worked on the east coast and the west coast, and the figures used are standard for the industry.

Property Tax: 1.25% of the sales price divided by 12 = monthly property tax.

Property Insurance: 0.50% of the loan amount divided by 12 = monthly property insurance.

RATIOS

Ratio Guidelines: 33% Top / 36% Bottom

The ratio is a system the mortgage banking industry uses to determine if the requested loan amount is affordable to the home buyer. The system measures your income to total debt owed.

Top Ratio includes - Total Housing Expense

- Principal and interest payment.

- Property tax.

- Homeowners insurance (excluded on condo).

- Flood insurance (only if in flood zone).

- HOA Dues - Condo or Pud.

- PMI (if less than 20% down payment).

Bottom Ratio includes installment debt with more than 10 months payments remaining and all revolving debt. Any debt not showing on the credit report, such as child support payments or alimony payments, is also included in the bottom ratio.

Bottom Ratio includes - Total Housing Expense Plus the Following:

- Installment debt with more than 10 months payments remaining.

- Revolving charges, minimum payment from credit report.

- Student loans that are not deferred.

- Child support payments and/or alimony payments.

Not Considered in the Ratios:

- Auto loan or other installment debt with 10 payments or less remaining.

- Revolving charge cards paid in full each month, such as gas cards.

- Student loans that are deferred for at least one year.

It is always better to have a high bottom ratio than a high top ratio. The top ratio is fixed for the term of the loan, where as the bottom ratio debt will change from bills having the ability to be paid off.

Charge-offs, collections, tax liens, or other liens need to be paid off prior to the closing of your home loan. Medical collections may be the exception if there is an insurance issue. We all know that insurance companies are notorious in paying late or just being difficult.

Keep in mind, the ratios are only a guideline, and can be exceed with good compensating factors.

Good Compensating Factors Include:

- High credit score.

- Excellent cash reserves.

- Low loan to value (LTV).

- Income, such as bonus income or overtime not considered in the ratios.

- Military income not considered in the ratios.

- Professional person just starting career such as Physician or Attorney.

- Minute credit user, shows respect for credit.

Credit History

As was mentioned in the credit report chapter, your credit score is the single most important factor in obtaining conventional financing. The credit score will determine the type of loan program you will qualify for and the interest rate you will be required to pay. The better your credit score, the more favorable interest you will be able to receive. It all boils down to risk factor.

The lender is looking for reasonably good credit. The borrower needs to be credit worthy. The credit report says volumes about a person's character and that is why a lot of employers are pulling credit reports on job applicants these days.

Late Payments: (30, 60, 90 days late)

Several 30-day late payments on your credit cards should not hurt you, but if payments are 60 or 90 days late, the lender will definitely have a problem lending you money. If you have a 90-day late payment and you can document that the debt is in dispute for some reason, the situation might be acceptable to the lender.

The payment history on your home or apartment is most important to a lender. It must be clean, with no late payment in the last 12 months. Whether you are presently renting or are making mortgage payments, it is imperative the housing expense is paid on time.

Collections, Tax Liens or Judgements:

Unless these are medical, they need to be paid off prior to or at the closing of your loan. Don't take it upon yourself to pay the debt off if your loan is in processing unless you can be sure there is time for the lender to verify the debt has been satisfied. Allow the debt to be paid through closing, and your loan processor will advise you on what to do.

Medical collections are another matter. They do not need to be paid off to close your loan. Medical insurance companies are notorious for paying medical bills late, or they dispute what they will cover. For this reason, lenders understand there is a problem with the medical insurance industry, and will allow you to arbitrate and settle medical matters yourself.

Bankruptcy:

Chapter 7 - is asking the courts to dissolve all your debt. The available assets do not cover the debt owed. Three years must have lapsed since the discharge of the bankruptcy and the borrower must have re-established good credit for a mortgage loan consideration.

Chapter 13 - is very different from chapter 7. The party filing for bankruptcy is not asking to have their debts dissolved, instead, they are asking for re-organization with the help of the courts. Same guidelines as Chapter 7, but I will tell you, as an underwriter, that I look at a borrower who files for Chapter 13 in a much more favorable light than someone who files for Chapter 7. The borrower who files Chapter 13 is not shrugging responsibilities. Chapter 13 debtor will pay the debt off in time through the courts instead of having it written off.

Foreclosure:

Seven years must have lapsed since a property foreclosure was discharged before a borrower can qualify for a home loan again. The mortgage industry caused havoc with people, by giving them loan programs that people could not pay. I am sure the seven-year guideline will probably change very soon, since the industry caused a foreclosure problem for a lot of people with our current state of affairs.

Authorized Signer:

An authorized signer on a credit card is an individual who is authorized to make purchases on a credit card, but is not responsible for repayment of the debt. This usually occurs in family situations, such as an elderly family member or a child in college. The debt shown on the credit report of an authorized user will not be included in the ratios, but the borrower will need to provide evidence of such.

INCOME

Qualifying income used for a home loan is your Gross Income, not the Net Income on your paycheck stub. Only the Veterans Administration qualifies a borrower using Net Income. We will cover that later in the VA section.

Typically, lenders require a two year history of income to qualifying for a home loan. Of course there are exceptions, such as young professional just out of college, doctor, lawyer, teacher, etc. In this case you will need to provide the lender with a copy of your degree and your two most current paycheck stubs. Let's say you are a new teacher who will start work in the new school year, and you have a contract reflecting your starting date. You will need to provide the lender with a copy of your contract for loan approval. If you do not have a paycheck stub at underwriting, the underwriter will condition the loan for you to bring a paycheck stub to the closing table reflecting the earnings on your contract. Sometimes these contracts absolve all or a portion of your student loans. In that case your student loans would not be counted in the ratios.

Reading Your Paycheck Stub:

- Weekly paycheck X 52 weeks divided by 12 = monthly income.

- Bi-weekly paycheck X 26 weeks divided by 12 = monthly income.

- Bi-monthly paycheck X 24 weeks divided by 12 = monthly income.

- Hourly Income X 2,080 hours divided by 12 = monthly Income.

Military Income: Along with a veterans military pay, the veteran can add military allowances, such as quarters and rations. Temporary pay such as Sea Pay or Flight Pay can only be considered a compensating factor.

Savings Interest Income: Average two years interest income from your 1040's, provided funds are not needed to close your loan.

Rental Income: You will need to provide the lender with two years of 1040's plus a Schedule E to show rental property income and expense.

Alimony and Child Support: Divorce decrees must be final and signed by the judge. The decree must show the payment will continue three years or more to be considered in the ratios.

Disability Income: Permanent disability income can be used to qualify for a home loan. You will need to provide a copy of the "Awards Letter" to the lender as evidence that you have three or more years remaining of disability income.

Trust Income: A copy of the trust will be needed to determine if the income can be used. The trust must be an "Irrevocable Trust" to be considered as income.

Retirement or Pension Income: Provide a copy of your retirement or pension papers to the lender as evidence you are receiving the income and that it will continue.

Self Employment Income: Two years of tax returns (1040's) with all schedules, and a current year-to-date profit and loss statement will be required to determine your income.

Partnership / Corporation: Two years of personal tax returns (1040's) will be needed along with two years of partnership returns (1065 forms) or corporate tax returns (1120 forms). Also, a current year-to-date profit and loss statement for the partnership or the corporation will be required

Teachers Income: A teachers contract is typically nine or ten months, depending on area. To determine monthly income, take contract wage and divide by 12 = monthly income. Some teachers choose to have their paychecks spread out over twelve months, while others like the higher pay over a nine month period. In the latter case, the pay must be divided by twelve for qualifying purposes.

Commission Income: This will be averaged over two years of income tax returns (1040's) with all schedules, minus expenses, taken from Schedule C from your 1040's.

Bonus Income: Averaged over two years If you have not received this income for two years, but received it last year and a letter from your company on company letterhead shows you will receive your bonus this coming year, it would be permissible to take your last year's bonus and average it over 24 months. This would be the most conservative approach and would give the borrower some of the bonus income for qualifying purposes.

Overtime Income: Averaged over two years. If overtime is more than 25% of your total income, you will need to provide two years of 1040's with all the appropriate schedules.

Social Security Income: Social Security income and some disability income are considered net income because it is not taxed. It is permissible to multiply your net income by 25% for qualifying purposes on a conventional loan and add that number to your income. This is called grossing up income.

Example:

$1000.00 X 25% = $250.00, added to $1,000.00 = $1,250.00 qualifying income.

Second Job Income: You must have held a second job for two consecutive years to use the income for loan qualifying. If less than two years, the second job income becomes a compensating factor to offset higher ratios.

Funds To Close Your Loan

Whether you are making a large or small down payment, the funds to close will need to be verified. Two of your most recent bank statements will be required to verify you have sufficient funds to close your loan. The assets verified must also include two months of house payments for reserves. With the lender meltdown, I am sure the written verification of deposit may return very soon. The verification of deposits is mailed to your bank to support the bank statements.

Lenders will question any large deposits that do not support your earnings. They want to be sure you did not take out a loan for the down payment to buy your home.

In the past, lenders required that borrowers have at least 5% of their own funds in the property. You can have a gift of money from a relative for the remainder of the down payment. Lenders are still requiring that borrowers have a reasonable amount of their own funds in the property.

Gift Letter: A gift letter will be required from the donor. Your gift can be from mom, dad, grandma, grandpa, aunt or whoever, as long as they are a relative giving the gift. Also, a bank statement from the donor of the gift is needed to show they have the ability to give the gift. Prior to closing your loan, a clear trail must show the transfer of the gift from the donor's account to your account, a cashier's check from the donor's account or to the closing agent.

Steps To Avoid

Once you complete your loan application, do not make any changes to your financial position.

- Do not change your employment if you can help it. If a job change is unavoidable, you must stay in the same line of work and earn the same wage or more if ratios are tight. Let your loan processor know immediately.

- Be sure not to increase your debt.

- Do not transfer credit card balances to new credit cards.

- Do not open new credit cards.

- Do not make any large purchases such as a car or furniture your new home while your loan is in process.

- Do not move your money at the bank. Just leave it alone until the closing of your loan. These funds need to be verified. This is a common mistake when moving to another city or state. The funds can stay in the state you are leaving and can be wire transferred at closing.

CHAPTER 6

REFINANCING YOUR CONVENTIONAL LOAN

As this is being written, our President is urging the American people to take advantage of low interest rates to refinance their property. This is how out of touch Washington is with the people of our country. Mr. President, don't you think if I could refinance my property and lower my house payment, I would?

The lending institutions will not work with people, even though they promised they would do so, while having their hands out and taking billions of dollars in taxpayer money. Mean while, property values have declined. Many people made a down payment of 20% or more on their properties to avoid PMI insurance. With property values declining, PMI insurance would now be required to refinance one's property. By the time you add the PMI insurance premium on your new refinanced payment, you are not saving a dime. In some cases the payment will be higher than before you refinanced.

The lenders could refinance your loan without PMI if they were serious about working with people. They did get special commitments from Fannie Mae and Freddie Mac, to refinance those loans that were sold to Fannie or Freddie. But what about the rest of us whose loans were not sold to Fannie or Freddie. If a lender already has your loan and the loan originated without PMI insurance because you had a large down payment, the lender could easily modify the interest rate and the term of the existing loan with not much skin off the their nose.

But the lenders simply do not want to take a risk, although it seems to me to be a much bigger risk not to. It may come to a point when people will realize they are putting good money out for bad. They may decide to leave the keys on the kitchen counter and walk out, never to return. It has happened in the past during the 1980's, when people did just that in certain parts of the country. I am sure the lenders do not want a bunch of houses on their books. There has been talk of lenders reducing the loan balances because of the declining values. That would be insane. I don't feel the lender owes me or anyone else for the declining property values. All I ask is that they please work with us and give their good customers the help they deserve, just as they were helped with our tax money.

When Should You Refinance?

There are so many factors that go into answering that question. Most likely it is to lower your interest rate. The big question is, is it worth it? For example:

Present Loan: $100,000 Loan Amount @ 6% = $599.56

New Loan: New Interest Rate @ 5% = $536.82

The borrower is saving $62.74 per month. But it will cost about $3,500 to refinance, and will take the borrower almost five years to recover the refinance charges. Is it worth it?

Let us look at another example with a much higher loan amount:

Present Loan: $400,000 Loan Amount @ 6% = $2,398.20

New Loan: New Interest Rate @ 5% = $2,147.28

This borrower is saving $250.92 per month. The cost of the refinance is $5,200 and will be recovered in 21 months. It makes perfect sense for the borrower to refinance to a lower interest rate.

Another reason to refinance might be, to combine your first and second mortgage together. The interest rates on junior liens are typically much higher than first mortgages. Whatever the reason you may want to refinance your property, do your homework first. You might be lucky enough to be with a lender that has a refinance program where you do not need to re-qualify for the loan. In that case, you would apply for your refinance with your original lender.

Most lenders have really tightened up on the amount of money they are willing to lend. If you need higher than 90% loan to value for a rate and term refinance, at this time you might have difficulty finding it.

- Rate and Term Refinance – Would be refinancing your mortgage loan with no cash back. Up to 90% loan to value, you might find a lender willing to take a 95% loan to value.

- Cash Out Refinance: 80.0% or less loan to value

Refinancing With a Junior Lien

A junior lien is any lien below the first mortgage. Combining the first mortgage along with the second mortgage or the equity line will be considered a rate and term refinance, as long as the second mortgage or the equity line has been open for 12 months or longer. The equity line of credit cannot have had any draws over $1,000 in last 12 months. If the junior lien has been opened less than 12 months, the new loan will be considered a cash out refinance. Let us look at an example of combining the first and second mortgages together with a new refinance.

Present Loan: $200,000 1st Loan Amount @ 6%   = $1,199.11

$50,000 2nd Loan Amount @ 7.5% =   349.50

Total Payment $1,548.61

New Payment: 1st mortgage $250,000 @ 5.5% interest = $1,419.45

A monthly savings of $129.16 is realized by combining the first and the second mortgage. It will take about 30 months to recoup the refinance fees. The borrower no longer has a second mortgage on the property, and the borrower is free to add an equity line of credit if he so desires.

Sometime lenders run specials. They will refinance you're property with little or no cost to you, just to get your loan. These specials weigh heavily upon market conditions. Credit Unions are more likely to offer no cost loans. I want to clarify, no cost loans actually means no lender costs, there will still be some cost in a "no cost" loan, such as Title search, Recording fees, Tax stamps, Reconveyance fee, Survey and Appraisal fee.

To start you're loan refinance, you will need to pay for your credit report and the appraisal fee up front. The cost to start your refinance should be $450.00 - $500.00 for conforming loan limits. Jumbo loans require higher appraisal fees, depending on the size of the property. Certain types of Jumbo loans require two appraisals. The credit report fee and the appraisal fee are non-refundable fees.

NOTES

CHAPTER 7

THE FHA LOAN

Who is FHA?

The Federal Housing Administration (FHA) is a division of the Department of Housing and Urban Development (HUD). In 1934, in an effort to lift the United States out of the great depression, President Franklin D. Roosevelt created the Federal Housing Administration (FHA) to insure private home improvement loans for middle income families. In 1938 FHA became a home building agency as well.

FHA insured loans are not supported by tax dollars as many people believe. Borrowers actually fund the loans themselves, through a mortgage insurance fund.

The Mortgage Insurance Premium Fund, otherwise known as MIP, is what FHA charges the borrower in obtaining an FHA loan, except for condominium properties. The up-front MIP is added to your loan amount and is a one time fee. The fee goes into the Mutual Mortgage Fund. The Mutual Mortgage Insurance (MMI) is monthly and is added to your monthly house payment. This fee also goes into the Mutual Mortgage fund. Condo properties are exempt from the up-front MIP but condo properties do pay the monthly MMI. I hope I did not scare you with these fees, because FHA is really a wonderful loan program.

At the present time, FHA has become a very popular loan program and with good reason. For first time home buyers, it is probably my favorite loan program. Lets look at some of the advantages of an FHA loan.

- An FHA loan is assumable.

- If interest rates decline, you get the benefit of a new lower rate with no out-of-pocket cost to you, and no qualifying through a Streamline Refinance without an appraisal.

- College students can buy what is called a "Kiddie Condo," but their parents must qualify for the mortgage.

- Loan only require a 3.50% down payment.

- 100% of the down payment can be gifted from a relative.

- Citizenship is not required. FHA will allow a Non-Permanent Resident Alien with a valid Social Security number and work visa.

- Cash reserves are not required at the closing of the loan.

- FHA accepts non-traditional credit if the borrower has not established credit.

- FHA does not have occupant ratios when a co-borrower is used, except when the primary borrower has not established a credit history.

During the housing boom from 2000 through 2006, many people with less than desirable credit were shifted into sub-prime loans. These same people should have been offered FHA financing before being thrown to the wolves. FHA is forgiving on derogatory credit when a good letter of explanation is provided.

An ethical loan agent will always have your best interest at heart. But, some loan agents were responsible for the sub-prime loans sold in the past several years. Unethical agents took the easy way to turn loans for fast returns of their commissions with no regard for you or me.

Borrowers who relied on loan agents to give their best when needed, were sitting ducks. It was pitiful, and those agents know who they are. I hope they can sleep at night. I am just one person, but I care enough to write this book in the hope that this deplorable meltdown of our economy never happens again. It is imperative that you use a loan agent who is seasoned in conventional loans, as well as government loans, and that the agent knows the guidelines for the loan products they are selling.

My young cousin in Ohio just finished his residency in podiatry and he sort of put the cart before the horse. He opened his podiatry office and two months later wanted to buy a condo. It should have happened the other way around, while he was in his residency. He went to the local bank and made application for an FHA loan, at my advice. I told him his dad would need to co-sign the loan. The bank turned my cousin down because he had just opened his podiatry office. He did not have the required time as a self-employed borrower. I would have agreed with that decision if the loan was a conventional loan. FHA guidelines were not exercised by the bank.

The loan agent did not do his job. The agent was selling FHA loans, but was not familiar with the program.

FHA does not have occupant ratios. Occupant ratios are when a co-mortgagor is present. The occupants income must support the ratio guideline, without the co-mortgagor. With FHA financing, both incomes are used to qualify the borrower. As long as the occupant borrower has good credit established, a family member can co-sign for the loan, and FHA will take the ratios from the co-signer's income along with the occupant borrower. The home will be in the borrower's name as well as that of the co-signer.

My cousin and his dad went to another bank and got the loan because the second bank was knowledgeable of FHA guidelines. Don't give up if you are turned down by a lender. Maybe the agent is not well versed on government guidelines, try another.

FHA loans are put through the Automated Underwriting System, this is called "FHA's Total Scorecard". The loan file is entered into the computer system and the computer will "Accept" or "Refer". The Refer means the computer did not approve the loan file, therefore it must be given to a DE Underwriter for manual underwriting. The borrower cannot be denied solely on the computer assessment.

FHA Loan Limits:

Effective November 7, 2008, HUD announced new FHA loan limits. The new loan limits will range from $271,050 to $625,500. Overall, the change in loan limits will help provide economic stability to America's communities. The maximum loan limit of $625,500 will only be applicable in extremely high cost metropolitan areas. Previously, FHA loan limits in these very high cost areas were capped at $362,790.

Special exceptions for Alaska, Hawaii, Guam and the Virgin Islands offer a higher ceiling of $938,250 for a single family residence.

Loan limits are based on the county where you want to purchase your home. The loan limits vary throughout the country. There are high cost areas and low cost areas. Your local lender who is FHA approved can give you the loan limits for the area where you wish to purchase your home.

FHA has expanded its regional offices in the U.S. from five to ten regional offices. Each of these offices covers a combination of states. I have included HUD's directory for your convenience. If you would like more information regarding FHA loans, go to the web site www.hud.gov.

Determining The FHA Loan Amount

FHA requires a borrower to have a 3.50% down payment. The maximum loan to value is 96.50% of the sales price or the appraised value, the lesser of the two. FHA uses a Mortgage Credit Analysis Worksheet, otherwise known as the MCAW, to qualify a borrower for an FHA loan. In figuring the loan to value, the loan amount with MIP can never exceed the appraised value.

Here is an example based on a single family home, not a condo.

SALES PRICE:	**APPRAISED VALUE:**
$218,000.00	$220,000.00

Maximum Loan Amount: $218,000.00 X 96.50% = $210,370.00

Up-Front MIP: X 1.75% = $3,681.48 (.48 cent paid in cash)
                                 _____

Total Loan Amount $214,051.00

Down Payment: $7,630.00

Once the appraisal is completed, and sent to the lender, the loan amount can change if the appraised value comes in under the sales price. In that case, your loan amount would be based on the appraised value, not the sales price if the seller will not adjust the sales price.

This example was done on a single family home. If this was a condo, simply omit the up-front MIP in determining your loan amount since condo's are exempt from up-front MIP.

UP-FRONT MIP:

On all FHA transactions with the exception of condos, the borrower pays an up-front MIP. Below is the fee chart for the up-front MIP. Calculate the percentage fee by your base loan amount, and then add that figure to your loan amount for your Total Loan Amount. Any cents will be paid in cash and not added to the total loan amount.

UP-FRONT MIP:

- PURCHASE TRANSACTION   1.75%

- CREDIT QUALIFYING REFINANCE   1.75%

- STREAMLINE REFINANCE   1.50%

- FHA SECURE   (Delinquent Borrowers)   3.00%

Even though condo owners are exempt from up-front MIP, they do pay the monthly MMI.

MONTHLY MMI PREMIUM:

As explained earlier, the Mutual Mortgage Insurance fund is the fund that helps keep FHA solvent. The borrower pays this fee each month with their house payment and the lender then pays it at the end of the year, just as your property taxes and insurance are collected. MMI is calculated from your base loan amount, not your loan amount with MIP.

Use the following chart to determine your MMI.

30-YEAR LOAN   95.% OR HIGHER LTV - .55%

                                                   UNDER 95% LTV - .50%

15-YEAR LOAN   90.% OR HIGHER LTV -.25%

                                                   UNDER 90% LTV - NONE

FHA SECURE   **(delinquent borrowers)**

                                                  95.% OR HIGHER LTV - .55%

                                                  UNDER 95.% LTV - .50%

Refunds of Up-Front MIP:

When your FHA loan is paid off through a refinance or the sale of your property in the first three years of the loan, you are entitled to a partial refund of your up-front MIP you paid when you purchased your home. After three years, there is no refund, except for those loans that closed prior to December 8, 2004. For loans that closed prior to December 8, 2004, the borrower is entitled to as partial refund for seven years, contact your loan processor or HUD if you fall in the latter category. The chart shows the percentage of the paid up-front MIP you should receive back.

Refund Chart For Loans Closed After December 8, 2004

Up-Front Mortgage Insurance
Premium Refund Percentages

Month of Year

YEAR	1	2	3	4	5	6	7	8	9	10	11	12
1	80	78	76	74	72	70	68	66	64	62	60	58
2	56	54	52	50	48	46	44	42	40	38	36	34
3	32	30	28	26	24	22	20	18	16	14	12	10

Sales Concessions:

Sales concessions are inducements to purchase the property from the seller, real estate agent, builder or any other interested party to the transaction. A sales concession exists, when personal property or closing cost are valued six percent or more of the sales price. In that case, the sales price is reduced dollar for dollar in determining the loan amount. That would result in a larger down payment for you. The sales price is not really reduced, only for loan purposes.

FHA allows up to 6% of the sales price in concessions before the buyer needs to subtract from the sales price for loan purposes only. Each dollar exceeding 6% must be deducted from the sales price, resulting in more cash out of pocket.

- **SALES CONCESSIONS ARE -** discount points, buy-down of the interest rate, prepaid escrows and closing cost paid by the seller. Personal property such as riding lawn mower, furniture and decorating allowance.

- **NOT A SALES CONCESSION -** Ranges, refrigerator, dishwasher, washer and dryer as well as carpeting or flooring allowance or window treatments.

It is important that your purchase contract is written correctly so it will not cause you to come to the closing needing more money. In essence, a carpet allowance and a decorating allowance mean the same thing, but the end result can be very different. A carpeting allowance is not a sales concession, but a decorating allowance is a sales concession.

Example of a Sales Concession:

To induce a sale, the seller agreed to $120,000 Sales Price and pay all the buyers closing cost, discount points, pre-paid escrows, and a decorating allowance. All toll, it was costing the seller $9,500. The allowable sales concession based on $120,000 Sales Price is $7,200. The difference being $2,300 must come off the sale price for loan purposes only, resulting in a larger down payment from the buyer. Had the sales concession not exceeded 6%, the borrowers down payment would have been $4,200 for this transaction.

Sales Price – $120,000 - $2,300 = $117,700.00

Adjusted Sales Price – $117,700 X 96.50% = $113,580.50

Down Payment – $6,419.50

Another scenario of a seller giving Cash or Gift Cards, is that the gift card must come off the sales price altogether because it was cash.

See the following example: a builder gave a $3,000 Gift Card, he would have served his buyer better by giving an Upgraded Floor, Window Treatments, Counter Tops, you get the idea. Without the gift card the buyer's down payment would have been $7,630.

Sales Price - $218,000.00 - $3,000. = $215,000.00

Adjusted Sales Price - $215,000.00 X 96.50% = $207,475.00

Down Payment - $10,525.00

CHAPTER 8

FHA TERMS AND GUIDELINES

- **ASSUMPTION:** FHA loans are fully assumable with credit approval.

- **CO-BORROWER:**   A non-occupant co-borrower is placed on an FHA loan to help the borrower qualify for the loan. FHA is the only loan product that does not have occupant ratios, as long as the occupying borrower has established good credit. Occupant ratio is the ratio for the occupying borrower when a Co-borrower is present. For example: your mother or father can qualify for the loan with you even though they will not be living in the property. A co -borrower must be a blood relative.

- **CREDIT ALERT SYSTEM (CAIVRS):**   A credit alert system is used by FHA and VA to determine if a borrower is in default on a government loan, such as a student loan.

- **ELIGIBLE PROPERTY:**   Property eligible for an FHA loan include a single family home, a 2-4 units property, and a Condo or PUD. For a Condo or PUD, the complex must be FHA or VA approved. A manufactured or mobile home is also eligible for FHA financing if the home is on its own land and is not in a mobile home park. The mobile home must display HUD'S certificate of conformity.

- **FEDERAL HOUSING ADMINISTRATION (FHA):** Is a loan program sponsored by the federal government and the department of Housing and Urban Development (HUD).

- **GOOD FAITH ESTIMATE:** The loan agent must give you a good faith estimate of all charges of your loan at the time of your loan application.

- **KIDDIE CONDO:** This program was designed for college students, but the parents qualify for the loan. This is a terrific loan in a hot real estate market. Once the young person is through with college, the proceeds from the sale of the condo would greatly off-set the high college tuition, and in some cases it exceed it.

- **LOAN ORIGINATION FEE:** A one time fee charged by the lender for the origination of the loan. FHA has limited this fee to 1% of the loan amount.

- **LOAN TO VALUE:** Sales price or appraised value, the lessor of the two is divided into the loan amount to determine the loan to value. The maximum loan to value on a purchase transaction or a credit qualifying refinance is 96.50%, and 85.0% loan to value is the maximum loan to value for a cash-out refinance.

- **MAXIMUM LOAN AMOUNT:** Based on county cost of living index, loan limits range from $271,050 to $625,500 for a single family home. The loan limits are based on high cost areas and low cost areas. You will need to call your local HUD office to find the loan limits for your area. Your real estate agent will also have that information. Two - four unit properties have higher loan limits accordingly.

- **MINIMUM DOWN PAYMENT:** As of January 1, 2009, the down payment for an FHA loan was raised to 3.50%.

- **MORTGAGE INSURANCE PREMIUM (MIP):** MIP is an insurance that was created to fund FHA loans. The up-front premium is paid into the Mutual Mortgage Insurance Fund. MIP is added up-front to the base loan amount. Condos are exempt from up-front MIP.

- **MUTUAL MORTGAGE INSURANCE (MMI):** Is what keeps FHA solvent. MMI is paid monthly with monthly mortgage payments on all FHA loans, including condos.

- **NON-PURCHASING SPOUSE:** When a spouse is not qualifying for the home loan. The credit report is still considered in a community property state. The credit report of the non-purchasing spouse will be included in the loan file and the debt of both parties will be used to qualify the loan.

- **OCCUPANCY REQUIREMENT:** To qualify for an FHA loan, the property must be an owner-occupied property by the borrower. A co-borrower need not occupy the property, and is on the loan merely to help credit qualify. Investors can purchase an FHA loan through foreclosures and the 203K rehabilitation program.

- **PRE-PAYMENT PENALTY:** FHA loans do have a pre-payment penalty. The penalty is 30-days interest on the loan at payoff. The reason is, FHA collects their interest in 30- day increment instead of per diem as VA and conventional.

- **RATIOS:** The FHA ratio guideline - **31.0% Top 43.0% bottom**. These ratios can be exceeded with good compensating factors, such as bonus income, second job, military allowances or other income not used to qualify the loan would be a compensating factor.

- **SALES CONCESSIONS:** When personal property is included with the property, the value cannot exceed 6% of the sales price or it becomes a sales concession. Any value more than 6% of the sales price, must be deducted dollar for dollar from the sales price, but that does not mean the sales price is reduced, it means you will need to come to closing with a higher down payment. Refer to what is a sales concession and what is not a sales concession.

- **SECONDARY FINANCING:** Most secondary junior liens on an FHA loan are from various government programs, such as the down payment assistance program or the Neighborhood Advantage program. If a junior lien is from the private sector, the following must be adhered to: 1) First and second mortgages cannot exceed a maximum loan to value, for your area; 2) Second mortgage cannot have a balloon payment sooner than five years; 3) Second mortgage must require monthly payments.

- **SECONDARY RESIDENCE:** FHA will allow a second FHA loan under extenuating circumstances. 1) Such as a job transfer too far to commute, usually 50 miles or more. 2) Divorce, 3) If family size has increased for size of home.

- **STREAMLINE REFINANCE:** Must presently have an FHA loan on the property. A borrower can refinance their property when the interest rate drops with no credit qualifying and no appraisal (in most states), with no out of pocket cost. These loans are done with an appraisal and without an appraisal, the criteria is different. See the Streamline Refinance section for clarification.

Most Commonly Used FHA Programs

- **203B - FIXED RATE:** The loan is fully amortized for 15 or 30 years, whatever term you chose. The payments are equal for the duration of the loan.

- **234C - CONDO:** This is a code HUD uses to identify a condo property from the others. The reason a condo has a separate code is because a condo does not pay up-front MIP.

- **203H - DISASTER VICTIM LOAN:** The disaster loan is created as a result of a disaster, such as Hurricane Katrina. It is a lower interest rate to help people recover from a disaster. 100% FINANCING IS AVAILABLE. Two to four unit properties do not qualify for the disaster victim loan. To qualify, the loan application must be delivered to the lender within one year of the disaster.

- **203K - REHABILITATION LOAN:** FHA will help a party interested in refurbishing a property located in urban areas or historical areas. You must provide drafting plans of your project to FHA for agency approval, and FHA will help finance the project with you. Investors can also apply for this program.

- **245 - GRADUATED PAYMENT MORTGAGE: (GPM):** A program where interest rate is bought down the early years of the loan, very much like a buy-down. The loan is qualified at the note rate, not the start rate.

- **251 - ADJUSTABLE RATE MORTGAGE (ARM):** ARM loans are qualified at the starting interest rate. The loans eligible for a FHA ARM loan are the 203B, 203H, 203K, and the 234C. FHA adjustable rate mortgage will be tied to one of the two indexes.

  1). The One Year London Interbank (LIBOR) or
  2). The One Year Constant Maturity Treasury (CMT).

1-Year ARM, 3-Year ARM, 5-Year ARM:

These loans are fixed for the period of time selected, either one, three or five years. ARM loans allow a 1.0% annual interest rate adjustment after the initial fixed interest rate period and a 5.0% cap over the life of the loan. These ARM loans are much more favorable than conventional ARM'S, because they cannot increase more than 1% for each adjustment period, and 5% for the life time of the loan.

7-Year ARM, 10-Year ARM:

These loans are fixed for 7 years or 10 years. After the fixed period these loans allow a 2.0% point annual interest rate adjustment, and a 6.0% cap over the life of the loan.

ARM LOANS: Frequency of interest rate adjustment, may occur no sooner than the following schedule;

- 1 Year ARM - No sooner than 12 months nor later than 18 months.

- 3 Year ARM - No sooner than 36 months nor later than 42 months.

- 5 Year ARM - No sooner than 60 months nor later than 66 months.

- 7 Year ARM - No sooner than 84 months nor later than 90 months.

- 10 Year ARM - No sooner than 120 months nor later than 126 months.

Calculate The New Adjusted Interest Rate:

The interest on an ARM loan is based on the current index (United States Treasury Securities) plus the margin, rounded to the nearest one-eighth of one percent point (0.125%). The calculated interest rate is used to determine the adjusted interest rate.

The "current index" refers to the most recent index figures available, 30 days before the change date. The Federal Reserve Board Statistical Release H-15 is published weekly on Monday, or Tuesday if Monday is a federal holiday. Compare the calculated interest rate (index + margin, rounded up to the nearest 1/8 of one percent point) to determine the new adjusted interest rate.

CREDIT ALERT SYSTEM (CAIVRS)

FHA started to use the Caivrs System about 15 years ago and the program was so successful, VA decided to join in utilizing the system a few years later.

What Is Caivrs? Caivrs is a system that shows if a person has ever defaulted on a government loan, whether it be from a student loan or an FHA or VA home loan. If a default shows up, the borrower will not be able to get a Caivrs number and without a Caivrs number, the borrower will not be able to qualify for a government home loan.

The loan processor will enter the borrower's Social Security number into the Caivrs system and if no outstanding delinquent debt on a government loan appears for the borrower, the loan file will be issued a Caivrs number. Without this number, the loan cannot be funded.

FHA Allowable Closing Cost

- Appraisal Fee.

- Attorney Fee or Escrow Fee (3rd party only).

- Credit Report.

- Courier Fees (refinance only and must be disclosed on the Good Faith Estimate).

- Discount Points (refinance and 203K loans only).

- Doc Stamps on Note / Mortgage / Deed.

- Doc Preparation Fee (3rd party only).

- Flood Certification.

- Home Inspection Fee.

- Intangible Tax on Mortgage or Deed.

- Manufactured Home Engineers Report.

- Name Affidavit Fee.

- Origination Fee (1% of base loan amount).

- Pest Inspection.

- Recording Fees for Deed and Mortgage.

- Repairs (if required by appraiser and contract states the buyer is to pay).

- Repair Escrow Fee (except on repossession or 203K loan).

- Survey.

- Tests or Treatments Required by HUD.

- Title Insurance / Endorsements and Title Search Fee.

FHA Non-Allowable Closing Cost

- Delivery Fee.

- Charge of HUD Case Binder.

- Disbursement Fee.

- Judgement Fee.

- Notary Fee.

- Photocopies.

- Re-Draw Document Fee.

- Processing / Transaction Fee.

- Transfer / Assignment of Mortgage.

- Tax Service Fee.

- Underwriting Fee.

- Warehousing Fee.

- Wire Transfer Fee.

HUD's Local Office Directory

State	Office Name/Address	Manager	Phone/ Fax	Region/Regional Office
AK	Anchorage Field Office 3000 C. Street Suite 401 Anchorage, AK 99503	COLLEEN K. BICKFORD Field Office Director	(907) 677-9800 Fax: (907) 677-9803 TTY: (907) 677-9825 Email	Region X Seattle WA
AL	Birmingham Field Office 950 22nd St North Suite. 900 Birmingham, AL 35203-5302	CINDY YARBROUGH Field Office Director	(205) 731-2617 Fax (205) 731-2593 Email	Region IV Atlanta GA
AR	Little Rock Field Office 425 West Capitol Avenue Suite 1000 Little Rock, AR 72201-3488	ALICE RUFUS Field Office Director	(501) 324-5931 Fax (501) 324-6142 Email	Region VI Ft. Worth TX
AZ	Phoenix Field Office One N. Central Avenue Suite 600 Phoenix, AZ 85004	REBECCA FLANAGAN Field Office Director	(602) 379-7100 Fax (602) 379-3985 Email	Region IX San Francisco CA
AZ	Tucson Field Office 160 North Stone Avenue Tucson, AZ 85701-1467	PHYLLIS LIM Field Office Director	(520) 670-6000 Fax (520) 670-6207 Email	Region IX San Francisco CA
CA	San Francisco Regional Office 600 Harrison St. 3rd Floor San Francisco, CA 94107-1300	CAROLINE H. KREWSON Deputy Regional Director	(415) 489-6400 Fax (415) 489-6419 Email	Region IX San Francisco CA
CA	Fresno Field Office 855 M Street Suite 970 Fresno, CA 93721	ROLAND SMITH Field Office Director	(559) 487-5033 Fax (559) 487-5191 Email	Region IX San Francisco CA
CA	Los Angeles Field Office 611 W. Sixth Street Suite 800 Los Angeles, CA 90017	RAY BREWER Field Office Director	(213) 894-8000 Fax (213) 894-8110 Email	Region IX San Francisco CA
CA	Sacramento Field Office John E. Moss Federal Building Room 4-200 650 Capitol Mall Sacramento, CA 95814	CYNTHIA L. ABBOTT Field Office Director	(916) 498-5220 Fax (916) 498-5262 Email	Region IX San Francisco CA
CA	San Diego Field Office Symphony Towers 750 B Street Suite 1600 San Diego, CA 92101-8131	FRANCIS X. RILEY Field Office Director	(619) 557-5310 Fax (619) 557-5312 Email	Region IX San Francisco CA
CA	Santa Ana Field Office Santa Ana Federal Building Room 7015 34 Civic Center Plaza Santa Ana, CA 92701-4003	RAY BREWER Acting Field Office Director	(714) 796-5577 Fax (714) 796-1285 Email	Region IX San Francisco CA

HUD's Local Office Directory

CO	Denver Regional Office 1670 Broadway, 25th Floor Denver, CO 80202	DEBORAH GRISWOLD Deputy Regional Director	(303) 672-5440 Fax (303) 672-5004 Email	Region VIII Denver CO
CT	Hartford Field Office One Corporate Center 20 Church Street 19th Floor Hartford, CT 06103-3220	JULIE FAGAN Field Office Director	(860) 240-4800 Fax (860) 240-4850 Email	Region I Boston MA
DC	Washington, DC Field Office 820 First Street NE Suite 300 Washington, DC 20002-4205	JOHN E. HALL Field Office Director	(202) 275-9200 Fax (202) 275-9212 Email	Region III Philadelphia PA
DE	Wilmington Field Office 920 King Street Suite 404 Wilmington, DE 19801-3016	DIANE LELLO Field Office Director	(302) 573-6300 Fax (302) 573-6259 Email	Region III Philadelphia PA
FL	Miami Field Office 909 SE First Avenue Miami, FL 33131	ARMANDO FANA Field Office Director	(305) 536-5678 Fax (305) 536-5765 Email	Region IV Atlanta GA
FL	Jacksonville Field Office Charles E. Bennett Federal Building 400 W. Bay Street, Suite 1015 Jacksonville, FL 32202	J. NICHOLAS SHELLEY Field Office Director	(904) 232-2627 Fax (904) 232-3759 Email	Region IV Atlanta GA
FL	Orlando Field Office 3751 Maguire Boulevard Room 270 Orlando, FL 32803-3032	PAUL C. AUSLEY, JR. Field Office Director	(407) 648-6441 Fax (407) 648-6310 Email	Region IV Atlanta GA
FL	Tampa Field Office 500 Zack Street Suite 402 Tampa, FL 33602	KAREN JACKSON SIMS Field Office Director	(813) 228-2026 Fax (813) 228-2431 Email	Region IV Atlanta GA
GA	Atlanta Regional Office 40 Marietta Street Five Points Plaza Atlanta, GA 30303-2806	PAT HOBAN-MOORE Deputy Regional Director	(404) 331-5001 Fax (404) 730-2392 Email	Region IV Atlanta GA
HI	Honolulu Field Office 500 Ala Moana Blvd. Suite 3A Honolulu, HI 96813-4918	GORDAN FURUTANI Field Office Director	(808) 522-8175 Fax (808) 522-8194 Email	Region IX San Francisco CA
IA	Des Moines Field Office 210 Walnut Street Room 239 Des Moines, IA 50309-2155	BRUCE RAY Field Office Director	(515) 284-4512 Fax (515) 284-4743 Email	Region VII Kansas City KS
ID	Boise Field Office Plaza IV, Suite 220 800 Park Boulevard Boise, Idaho 83712-7743	WILLIAM JOLLEY Field Office Director	(208) 334-1990 Fax (208) 334-9648 Email	Region X Seattle WA

HUD's Local Office Directory

IL	Chicago Regional Office Ralph Metcalfe Fed Building 77 West Jackson Boulevard Chicago, IL 60604-3507	BEVERLY BISHOP Deputy Regional Director	(312) 353-5680 Fax (312) 886-2729 Email	Region V Chicago IL
IL	Springfield Field Office 500 W. Monroe St., Suite 1 SW Springfield, IL 62704	JOHN W. MEYERS Field Office Director	(217) 492-4120 Fax (217) 492-4154 Email	Region V Chicago IL
IN	Indianapolis Field Office 151 North Delaware Street Suite 1200 Indianapolis, IN 46204-2526	JOHN HALL Field Office Director	(317) 226-6303 Fax (317) 226-6317 Email	Region V Chicago IL
KS	Kansas City Regional Office 400 State Avenue Room 507 Kansas City, KS 66101-2406	GENE LIPSCOMB Deputy Regional Director	(913) 551-5462 Fax (913) 551-5469 Email	Region VII Kansas City KS
KY	Louisville Field Office 601 West Broadway Louisville, KY 40202	KRISTA MILLS Field Office Director	(502) 582-5251 Fax (502) 582-6074 Email	Region IV Atlanta, GA
LA	New Orleans Field Office Hale Boggs Federal Building 500 Poydras Street, 9th Floor New Orleans, LA 70130	MARVEL ROBERTSON Field Office Director	(504) 589-7201 Fax (504) 589-7266 TTY: (504) 589-7277 Email	Region VI Ft. Worth TX
LA	Shreveport Field Office 401 Edwards Street Room 1510 Shreveport, LA 71101-5513	MARTHA SAKRE Field Office Director	(318) 226-7030 Fax (318) 676-3506 Email	Region VI Ft. Worth TX
MA	Boston Regional Office 10 Causeway Street Room 301 Boston, MA 02222-1092	KRISTINE FOYE Deputy Regional Director	(617) 994-8200 Fax (617) 565-6558 Email	Region I Boston MA
MD	Baltimore Field Office 5th Floor 10 South Howard Street Baltimore, MD 21201-2505	JAMES KELLY Field Office Director	(410) 962-2520 Fax (410) 209-6670 Email	Region III Philadelphia PA
ME	Bangor Field Office 202 Harlow Street - Chase Building Suite 101 Bangor, ME 04401-4919	WILLIAM D. BURNEY Field Office Director	(207) 945-0467 Fax (207) 945-0533 Email	Region I Boston MA
MI	Detroit Field Office 477 Michigan Avenue Detroit, MI 48226-2592	LANA J. VACHA Field Office Director	(313) 226-7900 Fax (313) 226-5611 Email	Region V Chicago IL
MI	Flint Field Office Phoenix Building 801 South Saginaw, 4th Floor Flint, Michigan 48502	Vacant Field Office Director	(810) 766-5112 Fax (810) 766-5122 Email	Region V Chicago IL

HUD's Local Office Directory

State	Office	Director	Phone/Fax	Region
MI	Grand Rapids Field Office Trade Center Building 50 Louis Street, N.W. Grand Rapids, MI 49503-2633	LOUIS M. BERRA Field Office Director	(616) 456-2100 Fax (616) 456-2114 Email	Region V Chicago IL
MN	Minneapolis Field Office Kinnard Financial Center 920 Second Avenue South Minneapolis MN 55402	DEXTER SIDNEY Field Office Director	(612) 370-3000 Fax (612) 370-3220 Email	Region V Chicago IL
MO	St. Louis Field Office 1222 Spruce Street Suite3207 St. Louis, MO 63103-2836	JAMES HEARD Field Office Director	(314) 539-6583 Fax (314) 539-6384 Email	Region VII Kansas City KS
MS	Jackson Field Office McCoy Federal Building 100 W. Capitol Street Room 910 Jackson, MS 39269-1096	CASSANDRA TERRY Field Office Director	(601) 965-4757 Fax (601) 965-4773 Email	Region IV Atlanta GA
MT	Helena Field Office 7 W 6th Ave Helena, MT 59601	TOM FRIESEN Field Office Director	(406) 449-5050 Fax (406) 449-5052 Email	Region VIII Denver CO
NC	Greensboro Field Office Asheville Building 1500 Pinecroft Road Suite 401 Greensboro, NC 27407-3838	CHRISTIAN STEARNS Field Office Director	(336) 547-4001 Fax (336) 547-4138 Email	Region IV Atlanta GA
ND	Fargo Field Office 657 2nd Avenue North Room 366 Fargo, ND 58108	JOEL MANSKE Field Office Director	(701) 239-5136 Fax (701) 239-5249 Email	Region VIII Denver CO
NE	Omaha Field Office Edward Zorinsky Federal Building 1616 Capitol Avenue Suite 329 Omaha, NE 68102-4908	CLIFTON JONES Field Office Director	(402) 492-3101 Fax (402) 492-3150 Email	Region VII Kansas City KS
NH	Manchester Field Office Norris Cotton Federal Building 275 Chestnut Street 4th Floor Manchester, NH 03101	GREG CARSON Field Office Director	(603) 666-7510 Fax (603) 666-7667 Email	Region I Boston MA
NJ	Newark Field Office One Newark Center 13th Floor Newark, NJ 07102-5260	DIANE JOHNSON Field Office Director	(973) 622-7900 Fax (973) 645-2323 Email	Region II New York NY
NJ	Camden Field Office Bridgeview Building 2nd floor 800-840 Cooper Street Camden, NJ 08102-1156	DIANE JOHNSON Acting Field Office Director	(856) 757-5081 Fax (856) 757-5373 Email	Region II New York NY
NM	Albuquerque Field Office 625 Silver Avenue SW Suite 100 Albuquerque, NM 87102	ELVA CASTILLO Field Office Director	(505) 346-6463 Fax (505) 346-6704 Email	Region VI Ft. Worth TX

HUD's Local Office Directory

NV	Las Vegas Field Office 300 S. Las Vegas Blvd. Suite 2900 Las Vegas, 89101-5833	KEN LOBENE Field Office Director	(702) 366-2100 Fax (702) 388-6244 Email	Region IX San Francisco CA
NV	Reno Field Office 745 West Moana Lane Suite 360 Reno, Nevada 89509-4932	TONY RAMIREZ Field Office Director	(775) 824-3703 Fax (775) 784-5005 Email	Region IX San Francisco CA
NY	New York Regional Office 26 Federal Plaza Suite 3541 New York, NY 10278-0068	JOANNA ANIELLO Deputy Regional Director	(212) 264-8000 Fax (212) 264-3068 Email	Region II New York NY
NY	Albany Field Office 52 Corporate Circle Albany, NY 12203-5121	ROBERT SCOFIELD Field Office Director	(518) 464-4200 Fax (518) 464-4300 Email	Region II New York NY
NY	Buffalo Field Office Lafayette Court 2nd Floor 465 Main Street Buffalo, NY 14203-1780	STEPHEN BANKO Field Office Director	(716) 551-5755 Fax (716) 551-5752 Email	Region II New York NY
NY	Syracuse Field Office 128 E. Jefferson Street Syracuse, NY 13202	ROBERT SCOFIELD Acting Field Office Director	(315) 477-0616 Fax (315) 477-0196 Email	Region II New York NY
OH	Columbus Field Office 200 North High Street Columbus, OH 43215-2463	THOMAS LEACH Field Office Director	(614) 469-2540 Fax (614) 469-2432 Email	Region V Chicago IL
OH	Cincinnati Field Office 632 Vine St. Fifth Floor Cincinnati, OH 45202	JAMES CUNNINGHAM Field Office Director	(513) 684-3451 Fax (513) 684-6224 Email	Region V Chicago IL
OH	Cleveland Field Office 1350 Euclid Avenue Suite 500 Cleveland, OH 44115-1815	DOUGLAS W. SHELBY Field Office Director	(216) 522-4058 Fax (216) 522-4067 Email	Region V Chicago IL
OK	Oklahoma City Field Office 301 NW 6th Street Suite 200 Oklahoma City, OK 73102	JERRY HYDEN Field Office Director	(405) 609-8509 Fax (405) 609-8588 Email	Region VI Ft. Worth TX
OK	Tulsa Field Office Williams Center Tower II 2 West Second Street Suite 400 Tulsa, OK 74103	RONALD MILES Field Office Director	(918) 292-8900 Fax (918) 292-8993 Email	Region VI Ft. Worth TX
OR	Portland Field Office 400 SW 6th Avenue Suite700 Portland, OR 97204-1632	ROBERTA ANDO Field Office Director	(971) 222-2600 Fax (971) 222-0357 Email	Region X Seattle

HUD's Local Office Directory

PA	Philadelphia Regional Office The Wanamaker Building 100 Penn Square, East Philadelphia, PA 19107-3380	BRENDA LAROCHE Deputy Regional Director	(215) 656-0500 Fax (215) 656-3445 Email	Region III Philadelphia PA
PA	Pittsburgh Field Office William Moorhead Federal Building 1000 Liberty Avenue, Suite 1000, Pittsburgh, PA 15222-2515	CHERYL E. CAMPBELL Field Office Director	(412) 644-6428 Fax (412) 644-4240 Email	Region III Philadelphia PA
PR	San Juan Field Office 235 Federico Costa Street Suite 200 San Juan, PR 00918	MICHAEL COLON Field Office Director	(787) 766-5400 Fax (787) 766-5995 Email	Region IV Atlanta GA
RI	Providence Field Office 121 South Main Street Suite 300 Providence, RI 02903-7104	NANCY SMITH Field Office Director	(401) 277-8300 Fax (401) 277-8398 Email	Region I Boston MA
SC	Columbia Field Office 1835 Assembly Street 13th Floor Columbia, SC 29201-2480	JIM CHAPLIN Field Office Director	(803) 765-5592 Fax (803) 253-3043 Email	Region IV Atlanta GA
SD	Sioux Falls Field Office 4301 West 57th Street Suite 101 Sioux Falls, SD 57108	SHERYL MILLER Field Office Director	(605) 330-4223 Fax (605) 330-4428 Email	Region VIII Denver CO
TN	Nashville Field Office 235 Cumberland Bend Suite 200 Nashville, TN 37228-1803	WILLIAM DIRL Field Office Director	(615) 736-5600 Fax (615) 736-7848 Email	Region IV Atlanta GA
TN	Knoxville Field Office 710 Locust Street, SW Suite 300 Knoxville, TN 37902-2526	MARK BREZINA Field Office Director	(865) 545-4370 Fax (865) 545-4569 Email	Region IV Atlanta GA
TN	Memphis Field Office 200 Jefferson Avenue Suite 300 Memphis, TN 38103-2389	JOHN GEMMILL Field Office Director	(901) 544-3367 Fax (901) 544-3697 Email	Region IV Atlanta GA
TX	Ft. Worth Regional Office 801 Cherry Street, Unit #45 Suite 2500 Ft. Worth, TX 76102	C. DONALD BABERS Deputy Regional Director	(817) 978-5965 Fax (817) 978-5567 Email	Region VI Ft. Worth TX
TX	Dallas Field Office 525 Griffin Street Room 860 Dallas, TX 75202-5032	BOB W. COOK Field Office Director	(214) 767-8300 Fax (214) 767-8973 Email	Region VI Ft. Worth TX
TX	Houston Field Office 1301 Fannin Suite 2200 Houston, TX 77002	EDWARD L. PRINGLE Field Office Director	(713) 718-3199 Fax (713) 718-3225 Email	Region VI Ft. Worth TX

HUD's Local Office Directory

TX	Lubbock Field Office 1205 Texas Avenue Room 511 Lubbock, TX 79401-4093	MIGUEL RINCON Field Office Director	(806) 472-7265 Fax (806) 472-7275 Email	Region VI Ft. Worth TX
TX	San Antonio Field Office One Alamo Center 106 South St. Mary's Street, Suite 405 San Antonio, Texas 78205-3625	RICHARD LOPEZ Field Office Director	(210) 475-6806 Fax (210) 472-6804 Email	Region VI Ft. Worth TX
UT	Salt Lake City Field Office 125 South State Street Suite 3001 Salt Lake City, UT 84138	DWIGHT A. PETERSON Field Office Director	(801) 524-6070 Fax (801) 524-3439 Email	Region VIII Denver CO
VA	Richmond Field Office 600 East Broad Street Richmond, VA 23219-4920	WILLIAM P. MILES Field Office Director	(804) 771-2100 Fax (804) 822-4984 Email	Region III Philadelphia PA
VT	Burlington Field Office 159 Bank Street 2nd Floor Burlington, VT 05401	MICHAEL MCNAMARA Field Office Director	(802) 951-6290 Fax (802) 951-6298 Email	Region I Boston MA
WA	Seattle Regional Office 909 First Avenue Suite 200 Seattle, WA 98104-1000	MARTHA DILTS Deputy Regional Director	(206) 220-5101 Fax (206) 220-5108 Email	Region X Seattle WA
WA	Spokane Field Office US Courthouse Building 920 W. Riverside, Suite 588 Spokane, WA 99201-1010	WILLIAM FATTIC Field Office Director	(509) 368-3200 Fax (509) 368-3209 Email	Region X Seattle WA
WI	Milwaukee Field Office 310 West Wisconsin Avenue Room1380 Milwaukee, WI 53203-2289	DELBERT REYNOLDS Field Office Director	(414) 297-3214 Fax (414) 297-3947 Email	Region V Chicago IL
WV	Charleston Field Office 405 Capitol Street Suite 708 Charleston, WV 25301-1795	PETER MINTER Field Office Director	(304) 347-7000 Fax (304) 347-7050 Email	Region III Philadelphia PA
WY	Casper Field Office 150 East B Street Room 1010 Casper, WY 82601-1969	DANBERRY CARMON Field Office Director	(307) 261-6250 Fax (307) 261-6245 Email	Region VIII Denver CO

Content current as of 15 September 2009

U.S. Department of Housing and Urban Development
451 7th Street, S.W., Washington, DC 20410

CHAPTER 9

QUALIFYING THE FHA LOAN

FHA Ratio Guidelines:

The standard Ratio is **31% Top ratio** to **43% Bottom ratio** of monthly gross income. There are differences in qualifying the FHA loan in relation to conventional financing. FHA is a lot more flexible in regard to credit standards, income used to qualify, and down payment money. The differences will be shown in this chapter regarding the standards for income, credit and funds to close your loan.

The direct endorsement underwriter can approve a loan exceeding guidelines with good compensation factors, FHA is very flexible. For example: if a borrower has not been on a second job for the required two-years and he needs to use the income to qualify, the underwriter cannot use the income for qualifying purposes. Although the underwriter can approve higher ratios' such as, 36% top / 48% bottom, as long as the underwriter can justify that decision, and in this case the underwriters justification is the second job income not being considered in the ratios.

Non-Traditional Credit: If a borrower has not established credit, non-traditional credit is acceptable with FHA. When a borrower has not established traditional credit such as revolving credit or installment credit, the borrower can still qualify for a home loan by using non-traditional credit, such as:

- A letter from your landlord reflecting your rent payment history.

- Statements from your utility companies showing your payment history.

- A letter from your union showing you are in good standing.

- A letter from your insurance agent that you pay your premiums on time.

Traditional Credit As Seen On The Credit Report:

30/60/90 DAY LATE PAYMENTS - These must be explained in the form of a letter in the loan file. A 30-day late payment, on your credit report, in reality is 60 days late. A late charge is not reported to the credit reporting agencies until a 30-day grace period has elapsed.

JUDGMENTS - A judgment must be paid off unless the borrower has been making regular payments on the judgment and the creditor is willing to subordinate to the new FHA loan.

COLLECTIONS - FHA does not demand that collections be paid off as a condition of the loan. However the lender might require it be paid off. FHA states, that if the collection is in dispute and you can provide documentation to evidence the dispute, then the loan can close without paying off the collection.

BANKRUPTCY - The bankruptcy should be discharged two years or more. It may be acceptable for loan approval with less than two years of the discharge, if the borrower can demonstrate the bankruptcy was beyond his control and no new derogatory credit has occurred since that time.

FORECLOSURE - Borrowers do not qualify for a new FHA loan if three years have not elapsed since the foreclosure. Exceptions can be made if the circumstances were beyond the borrower's control.

INCOME SOURCES :

Income used for qualifying an FHA loan is based on gross income as in conventional financing. FHA guidelines are very much like conventional guidelines with a few exceptions as shown in this chapter. FHA is a lot more liberal in underwriting guidelines, especially in regard to such things as time of receiving overtime or bonuses, and time on your job.

OVERTIME AND BONUS - Income can be used to qualify with as little as a 12-month history under certain circumstances. The borrower must provide evidence that the income will continue. FHA prefers a 24-month history, but it's guidelines are flexible.

SECOND JOB - The desired time for holding a second job is 24 months, but FHA will consider 18 months with a letter from the employer that the job will continue. For anything less than 18 months, the income for the second job becomes a compensating factor, where the underwriter can approve higher ratios, because the income from the second job is not considered in the loan.

SELF EMPLOYED - The borrower should have at least a two-year history of being self-employed. The borrower must provide two-years of personal tax returns (1040) with all schedules, and a current year-to-date profit and loss statement. Also two-years of partnership returns (1065) or two-years of corporate returns (1120), if applicable.

UNEMPLOYMENT COMPENSATION - This income can be used to qualify a borrower if the income is for seasonal workers, such as produce and fruit pickers. The borrower needs a history (at least two years) of this type of work and must show that he does collect unemployment compensation each year to consider it as income.

SOCIAL SECURITY - Social Security income is net income. Because it is net income, the income can be grossed up by 25% for qualifying purposes, for example:

Social Security income per month $1,550.00 X 25% = $387.50 added to benefits = $1,937.50 income for qualifying purposes.

RENTAL INCOME - This type of income can be used to qualify a borrower, as long as HUD's vacancy factor is included. The vacancy factor is set by the county where the property is located. Most counties use a 15% vacancy factor.

MILITARY RESERVES - Reserve income can be used if the borrower has at least two years time remaining in the reserves.

DISABILITY INCOME - This type of income can be used as long as a letter awarding the disability income is provided and the awards letter shows that the income will continue for three years or more.

CHILD SUPPORT OR ALIMONY INCOME - Income from child support and /or alimony can be used, if the final divorce decree is provided, and shows at least three years remaining income for child support and / or alimony.

MONTHLY LIABILITIES:

Installment debt - Borrowers are permitted to pay down installment debt to 10-months of remaining payments to eliminate the debt in qualifying for a loan. The exception would be if the new housing expense exceeds 50% of the borrower's present housing expense.

Revolving debt - The minimum monthly payment of a credit card reflected on the credit report will be added to the total monthly debt for qualifying ratios.

Child support payments - Child support payments will be counted in the ratio. The exception is, if a borrower has 10-months or less remaining on a child support obligation from loan closing.

Alimony - Because of the tax consequences of alimony payments, FHA permits the lender to treat the monthly alimony obligation as a reduction of the borrower's gross income in calculating the qualifying ratios, rather than as a monthly obligation. By working the loan in this manner can make a huge difference in the bottom ratio.

Projected Obligations - A borrower's student loan, for example, that will begin re-payment within 12 months from closing the new loan, will need to be counted in the ratios.

Contingent Liability - A contingent liability exists when an individual would be held responsible for payment of a debt for another party, if that party defaulted on the payment.

Co-Signed Obligations - If the borrower is a co-signer on an auto loan, a student loan, or any other obligation, contingent liability applies unless the borrower can provide documentation that the primary borrower has been making payments in a timely manner and that there have been no delinquent payments over the last 12 months.

Authorized Signer - This type of credit will not be counted in the ratios. An example would be, a borrower who is authorized to make purchases for a family member, but is not responsible for paying the account. This type of credit is common with senior citizens dependent on the help of their family members.

Non-Purchasing Spouse - A non-purchasing spouse is not on the loan application, even though they will occupy the property. In a community property state, the credit report of a non-purchasing spouse is to be included in the loan file and the debt is to be used in the ratio. However, this debt would not be a reason to deny the loan. This guideline is only on FHA loans.

Liabilities Not On Credit Report - These would include, but not be limited to a loan against your 401K, a loan through the military, child support or alimony. These types of personal loans or obligations would be considered in the ratio to qualify your loan.

FUNDS TO CLOSE

Typically, FHA is a lot more lenient in allowing other avenues for funds to close your new mortgage loan. All large deposits need to be supported by documentation to show where the large deposits came from, and are not borrowed funds.

Gift Funds - Funds from a gift can be 100% of the money needed to buy your home. The gift must be from a relative; a borrower's employer is acceptable if you can show a long term relationship, or a close friend as long as there is a clearly defined interest in the borrower. All must be documented. A family member may provide equity credit as a gift of property being sold to another family member. The donor of the gift may not have an interest in the sale of the property, such as a seller, a builder, a real estate brokers, etc. A letter from the gift donor will be required stating that no repayment is expected. A donor must show the ability to give the gift and must show a clear paper trail of the transfer of the gift to the borrower or closing agent.

Cash On Hand - This is acceptable as long as the borrower can adequately show the ability to save the money. Funds must be verified prior to closing the loan, such as opening a bank account. There are certain cultures that do not believe in banks, and they really do keep their money at home under the mattress.

Rent Credit - This would be found with a Rent-to-Purchase contract, or a Lease Option. The original rent-to-purchase contract would state what percentage of the monthly rent would go toward the purchase price if the tenant decides to purchase the property. The dollar amount that would be allowed for loan purposes is the cumulative amount of the rental payment that exceeds the appraiser's estimate of fair market rents paid.

If a tenant paid only fair market rent, then nothing would be considered the borrower's cash investment. Only the dollar amount that exceeds fair market rent can be used as the borrower's cash investment. The rent-with-option-to-purchase contract must have originated at the time the lease took place.

Qualifying A Tri-Plex or Four-Plex Property:

In qualifying a three or four unit property, FHA requires that the property support itself from the rent the property generates and cannot exceed 100%, of the principal, interest, taxes and insurance. We will go over examples: one property that supports itself and the loan is approved, and another scenario where the rents do not support the property and the loan is denied. The borrower must occupy one unit. The hypothetical rent for the borrower's unit can be used to support the building.

Net rental income is the appraiser's estimate of fair market rent, or the actual rent, the lessor of the two. You may use the appraiser's estimate for vacancy, or the vacancy factor used by the county jurisdiction, whichever is greater. The average vacancy factor is 15% on FHA loans.

FHA requires three months of reserves, principal, interest, taxes and insurance (PITI) after closing your loan. This requirement is for three and four unit properties only. The reserves must be from the borrower's own funds and cannot come from a gift or borrowed funds.

Let's say Mr. Mickey is retired and wants to buy a four unit property and live in one of the units. Mr. Mickey plans to make the minimum FHA down payment of 3.50%. His up-front MIP will be 1.75% and his monthly MMI will be 0.55%. Refer to the Up-Front MIP Chart and the Monthly MMI Chart in Chapter 7.

Four-Plex Example

Sales Price:	$210,000.00
Down Payment:	-7,350.00 = 3.50%

Loan Amount	$ 202,650.00 = 96.50% loan to value (LTV)
Up Front MIP	3,546.38 @ 1.75% (.38 cents paid in cash)

Total Loan Amount	$ 206,196.00 with MIP

Interest Rate @ 6% 30-year fixed.

Principal &Interest Payment (P&I)	$1,235.11
Property Tax	218.00
Hazard Insurance	85.00
MMI	92.88

Total House Payment (PITI)	$1,630.99

Example of A Property That Can Support Itself:

Monthly Rents Per Unit	$600.00 X 4 units =	$2,400.00
Less 15% Vacancy Factor		-360.00
Net Monthly Rents		$2,040.00

Monthly Mortgage Payments $1,630.99 divided by net rental $2,040 = 79.9 %. Does not exceed 100%, the property supports itself and the loan would be approved.

Example of A Property That Cannot Support Itself:

Monthly Rents Per Unit	$475.00 X 4 units =	$1,900.00
Less 15% Vacancy Factor		- 285.00
Net Rents		$1,615.00

Monthly Mortgage Payments $1,630.99 divided by net rental $1,615.00 = 100.9%. Exceeds 100%. The loan would be denied regardless of the ratios because property does not support itself.

Make Your Home Energy Efficient:

The Energy Efficient Mortgage (EEM) Program allows a borrower to finance 100% of the expense of the cost effective "Energy Package," the property improvement to make the house more energy efficient. The EEM Program recognizes that the improved energy efficiency of a house can increase its afford ability by reducing the operating cost. Energy efficiency improvements can include energy saving equipment, such as solar, energy efficient windows, Energy Star appliances and other active passive technologies. The costs can be added back into the loan. The maximum amount for the portion of the EEM for energy improvements is the lesser of 5% of:

- The value of the property, or

- 115% of the median area price of a single family dwelling, or

- 150% of the conforming Freddie Mac limit.

For Example: Mr. and Mrs. Mouse are purchasing a home valued at $300,000. They want to take full advantage of the EEM feature, which is $15,000 (5% of $300,000). They have decided to replace all the old windows with energy efficient windows and replace all the dated appliances with Energy Star appliances.

The current utility bills average $350 per month. Mr. and Mrs. Mouse contacted a certified Home Energy Rater and was given a report that the average savings would be $100 per month. The average life of the energy improvements is 15 years or 180 months. The energy savings over the life of the improvement will be $18,000. In this example, the base loan amount would be $304,500 ($300,000 X 96.50 + $15,000)

With an "Energy Efficient" loan, ratios can be exceeded by 2 points, and the reason is simple. Utility bills are greatly reduced when a home has been termed "Energy Efficient" compared to one that is not.

The EEM may be used for all property types, purchase and refinances transactions, including streamline refinances. New construction is also eligible. People really don't know this program exist, it is a wonderful program.

This a great opportunity to buy "green". Tell your Realtor or your loan agent that you would like to include the cost of energy-effective improvements with your mortgage. If they balk, please ask them to look into the program. If you are not happy with the answer, you will know they are not on-top of the guidelines, and you may want to take your business else where.

CHAPTER 10

FHA REFINANCE PROGRAMS

Rate and Term Refinance – A rate and term refinance involves refinancing existing debt on a loan and not taking any cash out of the property. For refinance transactions where case numbers are assigned after January 1, 2009, the maximum loan to value will be 97.75%.

If there is a second mortgage or equity line of credit on the property, and you want to consolidate it into one loan, you may be able to do that as long as the following conditions are followed. The subordinate lien must have been in place for 12 months or longer, otherwise, this would be considered a cash out refinance. If you are combining your equity line, there cannot have been any draws of more than $1,000 in the last 12 months. If there are large draws on an equity line and the money went back into the property for repairs, or updating the property, the loan would still be considered a rate and term refinance. Documentation will be needed to support the repairs.

TYPE OF REFINANCE	MAXIMUM LTV	UP-FRONT MIP
Rate and term	97.75%	1.75%
Streamline w/ Appraisal	97.75%	1.50%
Streamline w/o Appraisal	N/A	1.50%
Cash-Out Refinance	85%	1.75%

Existing Liens: Add together the unpaid principal balance of your first mortgage, any junior liens including an equity line of credit (with no draws over $1,000 in last 12 months) seasoned 12 months or longer. Loan amount permitting, you can add the closing cost, prepaid expenses, appraisal fee, discount points (if any), and any repairs the appraiser deemed necessary. Divide the total by the appraised value. The base loan amount not to exceed 97.75% of the appraised value, and the total loan amount with MIP, not to exceed 100% of the appraised value. Any amount over 100% of the appraised value needs to be paid in cash.

Example:

Appraiser's Estimate of Value: $220,000.00   **UF-MIP of 1.75%**

Maximum Mortgage before adding UF-MIP = $215,050.00

Maximum Mortgage with UF-MIP = $215,050 + $3,763 = $218,813

Loan to Value before Up-Front MIP: $215,050 divided into $220,000 = 97.750%

Loan to Value after Up-Front MIP: $218,813 divided by $220,000 = 99.460%

Subordinate Financing – A junior lien may remain in place regardless of when it was taken out, provided the FHA mortgage meets the criteria for secondary financing. The junior lien must be subordinate to the new FHA loan.

Qualifying For The Refinance – You will need to credit qualify for rate and term refinance or cash out refinance with full credit package and appraisal from an approved FHA appraiser. If your existing loan is an FHA loan and you are refinancing to a rate and term FHA loan, refer to the Streamline Refinance on the following page. This section will not apply to you.

Cash Out Refinance – You can take cash out up to 85% of the appraiser's estimate of value, including MIP. A loan amount with up front MIP cannot exceed 85% loan to value. The property must be owner occupied. If the property was purchased less than 12 months earlier, the loan amount would be determined by either the sales price of the property when purchased or the appraised value, the lessor of the two. All monthly payments must have been made in a timely manner, with no late payments in the last 12 months on your mortgage loan. Borrowers who are delinquent on their mortgage are not eligible for a cash out refinance. Only one or two unit properties are eligible for cash out refinances.

For high cost areas, over $417,00.00, two appraisals will be required on a cash out refinance. The second appraisal must also be by the FHA roster of appraisers. If the values differ between the two appraisals, the lowest value will be used to determine the new loan amount. **Maximum loan to value can never exceed 85% LTV on a cash out refinance.**

Borrowers With Late Mortgage Payments – Late payments on an FHA mortgage loan in the last 12 months will be limited to a Rate & Term refinance not to exceed 90% loan to value. A borrower can have up to three 30-day late payments or one 90-day late payment. This new refinance will be processed under the FHA Secure program, MIP is 3.0% on this program. FHA will consider modification of existing subordinate financing on this program. In addition to the maximum mortgage calculation, the new loan may include arrearage incurred because of interest rate reset or extenuating circumstances.

Streamline Refinance Program:

One of the wonderful features of having an FHA loan is the ability to reduce your interest rate without re-qualifying for a new loan when the market drops. FHA's theory, is that lowering your payment gives FHA more security. The Streamline Refinance may be done **with an appraisal** or **without an appraisal**. Very little documentation is required. The borrower is not to receive cash back at closing exceeding $500.00. You do not need to qualify for the Streamline Refinance, FHA feels you already qualified for the loan. You must have an FHA loan for a Streamline Refinance.

Refinance With An Appraisal: If done with an appraisal and credit report, all closing costs can be rolled into the new loan. The closing costs are limited and you will not need any out of pocket funds to close your loan. The Up-Front MIP on a Streamline Refinance is 1.50% of the loan amount, and added to the loan amount.

Refinance Without An Appraisal: When the Streamline Refinance is done without an appraisal, you will need to pay your closing cost out of pocket. If you are refinancing with your original lender, they might be able to transfer your escrow account to the new loan. In the event a transfer is not possible or you are refinancing through a different lender, remember you will be receiving a refund from the old lender from your escrow or impound account. Once you consider your refund, most people are paying less than 1.5% for the new loan.

Are you confused yet? The next page will clarify when you will need to credit qualify with an appraisal, and when you can refinance without credit qualifying or an appraisal.

Guidelines for an FHA Streamline Refinance - Without An Appraisal

- Mortgage current with no 30-day late payments in the last 12 months.

- Owner Occupied Only (except for the next item).

- Borrower who turned his property into a rental property must show he once lived in the property. Only the outstanding principal balance may be refinanced on a rental property. The remaining term of the mortgage plus 12 years, would be the maximum mortgage term. If the current mortgage has a remaining term of 17 years, then the new term could not exceed 29 years.

Guidelines for an FHA Streamline Refinance - With An Appraisal and Credit Qualify

- If monthly payment on the new loan exceeds 20% of the old loan, as a result of a change in the mortgage program, such as an ARM Loan to a Fixed Rate Loan, or change in the mortgage term, as a 30-Year Term to a 15-Year Term.

- Deletion of a borrower on the new loan, such as a co-signer.

- Following an assumption.

- Property transfer such as a divorce situation.

Types of Permissible FHA Streamline Refinances:

- No-Cost refinances.

- Refinancing to a shorter term mortgage.

- ARM to ARM refinancing.

- ARM to Fixed rate refinancing.

- Fixed rate to ARM refinancing.

- GPM to Fixed rate refinancing.

- GPM to ARM refinancing.

- Section 203K to Section 203B refinancing.

Other features of the Streamline Refinance include: FHA does not require a junior lien to be paid off, but it must subordinate to the new FHA loan, and FHA does not require work requirement reflected on the appraisal to be completed.

NOTE: Delinquent mortgages are not eligible for a Streamline Refinance.

NOTES

CHAPTER 11

WHAT IS THE VETERANS ADMINISTRATION?

The Veterans Administration (VA) is an independent agency which the federal government created with the Servicemen's Readjustment Act of 1944. During World War 11, numerous programs were created for veterans' including "The Zero Down Payment Home Loan Program."

Before the sub-prime fiasco of recent years, VA had the highest foreclosure rate in the mortgage industry. The reason is simple. The borrower on a VA loan had nothing invested in the property, so if times got tough the veteran would simply walk away from the home. The lenders knew this, yet they became more relaxed with these sub-prime loans and allowed people with poor credit to buy a home with little or no down payment. I am not going to spend time on sub-prime because that pitiful loan product has put our country in turmoil and don't kid yourself, it was all for money. This is precisely why I wrote this book and hope that in some small way I can be of help to home buyers.

In the late 1970's, during President Carter's administration, interest rates rose from 9% to 17%. In those days, if you wanted an FHA or VA loan, the loan package was processed by the lender of choice, and the processor shipped the loan package to VA or FHA.

I was a real estate agent at the time in Southern California. FHA was taking about 60-75 days for loan approval. VA, on the other hand, was taking as long as 90-120 days for loan approval. I was trying to earn a living, but I would have had better luck going to the race track. I know what you are thinking "What does she mean?"

Well, I'll tell you the way it was back then. Let's say a home buyer completed a loan application and the interest rate was 12% at the time. But with rates going up so fast at that time, and VA taking up to 120 days to approve a loan, when the home buyer finally received loan approval, the interest rate might be 15% or more, and not 12%. The home buyer no longer qualified for the loan or the payments were going to be so high, he or she no longer wanted the property.

By 1983, government agencies like FHA and VA, placed underwriting home loans directly with approved banks and saving and loans. The underwriters needed to be approved by both FHA and VA with extensive training. However, not all underwriters are government approved. In other words, underwriters' not only have a responsibility to their employer, but also to the government agency that approved them to underwrite government loans.

VA gave lenders the authority to approve the credit package only at that time, but required the appraisal to go back to VA. It was not until the early 1990's that VA gave underwriters approval to underwrite the entire loan package in-house including the appraisal.

VA Appraisal: **Certificate of Reasonable Value (CRV) - If you are planning on buying a home and using your VA Entitlement, this chapter will guide you through the process.**

The VA appraisal is the best and most reliable appraisal in the marketplace. The reason is simple. VA assigns the appraiser to the property and the lender has no control over who will be appraising the property. VA-approved, appraisers are on the VA appraiser's fee panel, but the appraisers actually were trained by VA in appraising property by VA standards.

Your loan processor will order your appraisal from VA instead of calling a real estate appraiser directly. The VA office will then go to its appraiser panel list and rotate an appraiser in your area.

For years, I felt all real estate appraisals should be ordered in a similar manner to ensure against a conflict of interest. This year that finally happened, the lenders can no longer dole out appraisal orders.

You will want to be sure your lender has a VA approved LAPP (Lender Appraisal Processing Procedure) underwriter on their staff. An underwriter receives the LAPP designation with training from VA, and the underwriter is nominated by the bank or saving and loan. In the event your lender does not have a LAPP approved underwriter, after the appraiser completes the appraisal, the appraiser will send the appraisal directly to VA for underwriting, a process which can take up to 30 days. You can see how important it is to ask the right questions.

Qualifying the VA loan – The VA loan is qualified differently then a conventional or FHA loan. VA considers only Total Debt Ratio and Remaining Residual for family support. Remaining Residual includes these major factors.

- Net income is used to qualify a VA home loan, not gross income. Taxes are taken off the gross income, and the underwriter can use the IRS tax charts, instead of the actual taxes paid, as shown on the borrower's paycheck stub.

- The VA Residual Income requirement must be meet also. Residual Income is the balance left for family support after the house payment PITI (principal, interest, taxes & insurance), utilities and remaining debt from the credit report are paid. VA has a residual chart for family size and loan amount.

Maximum Loan Limits – In 2009, the VA loan limit was increased to $417,000 for all counties except high cost areas. In the past, the loan limits were the same throughout the country, regardless of high cost areas. The loan limits do change from time to time, and I would suggest you go to the Veterans Administration web site to determine the maximum loan amount at the time of your purchase in your area. The web site, www.homeloans.vagov/eligibility.htm, also will give you other valuable information regarding your home purchase.

VA Loan Amount Calculations:

VA Purchase with Full Entitlement – The maximum VA zero down payment loan with full entitlement is $417,000.00 ($104,250.00 entitlement) inclusive of the funding fee.

VA Purchase Partial Entitlement – Calculate at 75% of the lesser of the sales price or the appraised value plus the remaining entitlement up to $417,000.00 inclusive of the funding fee.

VA Refinance – Use the lesser of the following formulas:
    #1.) 90% of appraised value, or

    #2.) 75% of the appraised value, plus remaining entitlement
        (Up to $417,000.00 inclusive of the funding fee)

VA Rate Reduction Refinance – When refinancing a currently insured VA loan, no cash back is allowed. The new loan can include the funding fee, discount points, loan origination fee and all closing cost.

VA Loans with Secondary Financing – Figure the lessor of 75% of the sales price or appraised value, plus the entitlement as the maximum total financing allowed by VA.

Example: Sales price of $450,000 X 75% = $337,500 plus entitlement of $104,250 = $441,750. The borrower needs to make an $8,250.00 down payment and the Second Lien is $24,750.00.

Certificate of Eligibility

A veteran will need a "Certificate of Eligibility" to obtain a VA Loan. The first step is to bring your "Certificate of Release from Active Duty," (DD214 form) to your local VA office, or to your loan agent if you do not have a VA office in your town. See Chapter 13 for VA offices in your area, or visit the internet web site for that information at:

www.homeloans.vagov/eligibility.htm

Your "DD214" must show an honorable discharge. A veteran with a dishonorable discharge from the service is not eligible for a VA home loan.

Once you submit your "DD214," the VA will issue your Certificate of Eligibility. Green is for past veterans, active duty soldiers and officers. Gold is for reservists and members of the National Guard.

The Certificate of Eligibility will show:

- The name of the eligible veteran.

- Amount of available entitlement.

- UNCONDITIONAL certificate means you have Full Entitlement.

- CONDITIONAL certificate means you have Partial Entitlement.

VA ENTITLEMENT

Who Is Entitled to a VA Loan?

- Any veteran who has completed 181 days of service.

- A present member of the military service.

- A veteran of WWII, the Korean War, the Vietnam War, the Persian Gulf conflict, the Middle East conflict, or the Iraq War. A veteran that served in war time must have completed 90 days of combat action.

- The unmarried spouse of a POW-MIA.

- A reservist or National Guard member who has completed a total of six years of selective service.

- Those who were discharged from the Reserves or National Guard because of a service connected disability before completing the required six years of service.

- An unmarried surviving spouse of a reservist who died from a service connected cause.

History of Veterans Entitlement

Veterans Entitlement is a term used by the veterans administration to refer to benefits available to a veteran obtaining a mortgage to buy a home. The amount of the entitlement is established by Congress. The entitlement is always 25% of the maximum loan limit. Currently the entitlement is $104,250.00 which could be used to buy a home worth four times the entitlement with no down payment or $417,000.00.

Changes In Entitlement Throughout The Years:

Original - 1930's	$2,000
September 16, 1940	$4,000
April 20, 1950	$7,500
May 7, 1968	$12,500
January 1, 1975	$17,500
January 1, 1978	$25,000
October 7, 1980	$27,500
February 1, 1988	$36,000
December 18, 1989	$46,000
September 16, 1996	$50,750
Present Time	$104,250 or higher for higher cost areas.

How To Compute Your Entitlement:

If you have never used your VA eligibility to buy a home, you can simply multiply the current maximum guaranty entitlement $104,250 X 4 = $417,000 would give you your maximum VA loan amount. I know this sound confusing, but to simplify it, just remember the Maximum Guaranty Entitlement is 25% of the Maximum Loan Amount for your area. The following examples illustrate some common situations involving VA loans.

Example 1. A veteran has full entitlement and is purchasing a home for $300,000 where the county loan limit is $417,000.

$417,000 X 25% = $104,250 maximum guaranty and available entitlement. This purchase will not require a down payment since the purchase price is less than the maximum loan amout.

Example 2. A veteran has full entitlement, but he is purchasing a home over county limit of $417,000. The purchase price of the home he is buying is $480,000.

Maximum loan limit $417,000 X 25% = $104,250 maximum guaranty and entitlement available $104,250 divided by $480,000 = 21.72%. Since the guaranty is less than 25%, the home buyer needs to make a down payment.

Sales Price $480,000 X 25% = $120,000

$120,000 - $104,250 (maximum guaranty) = $15,750

Required Down Payment = $15,750

Partial Entitlement – If a veteran has used a portion of his or her entitlement on another property and that VA loan is still outstanding, the veteran will only have a partial entitlement left. Maybe the veteran allowed his VA mortgage loan to be assumed and the buyer assuming the VA loan was not a veteran. As long as that loan is open it will tie up a portion of the veteran's entitlement.

Example 3. A veteran has used $48,000 of entitlement on a prior loan, which may not be restored and is purchasing a home for $320,000 where the county loan limit is $625,000.

$625,000 X 25% = $156,250 maximum guaranty

$156,000 - (used) $48,000 = $108,250 entitlement available

$108,250 X 4 = $433,000 maximum loan amount. No Down Payment Required.

Example 4. A veteran has used $36,000 of entitlement on a prior loan, which may not be restored, and is purchasing a home for $120,000 where the county loan limit is $417,000.

Since the loan amount will not be over $144,000. The veteran's additional entitlement cannot be used. Therefore, the guaranty would be 0%.

Restoration of Entitlement:

How To Restore Your Entitlement? The following conditions must be meet.

A) The property has been sold and the loan has been paid in full, or a qualified veteran transferee has agreed to assume the outstanding balance of the loan and agrees to <u>"Substitute Eligibility" for the same amount of entitlement originally used for the loan.</u> The assuming veteran must also meet the occupancy, income, and credit requirements.

B) A veterans' prior use of entitlement may be excluded, if the prior loan has been paid in full, and the veteran has made application for a loan secured by the same property. This includes the payoff of an existing VA loan by refinancing it with a conventional loan. This is where a lot of people get burned. Common sense would tell you, if a veteran paid off the VA loan through a conventional or FHA refinance, the veteran would have their entitlement back. WRONG! We are dealing with a government agency here and there is no common sense. You will need to sell the property. Read below.

C) ONE TIME ONLY – Because people could not wrap their brains around condition B, the above, VA came out with a one time exception. Your Certificate of Eligibility will show entitlement previously used in connection with (loan # 12345) has been restored if you refinance your home with a conventional loan. You can only take advantage of this one time on the same property.

What Is VA Funding Fee?

VA charges a one time fee called a funding fee, which goes into a fund to help keep VA solvent. Unless a veteran is exempt from paying a funding fee, the fee will be charged and will be added to the loan amount. If by adding the funding fee to the loan amount, the loan amount now exceeds the maximum loan limits, that dollar amount would need to be paid in cash. Use the chart on the next page for the funding fee charged.

Who Is Exempt From Funding Fee?

Disabled veterans are exempt from paying a funding fee. Your Certificate of Eligibility will show if you are exempt. If you have a pending disability compensation claim at the time of loan closing, the funding fee must be remitted as if you were not exempt. After the closing of your loan, you can contact the VA office to request a refund if it is later determined that you were entitled to compensation retroactive to a date prior to the loan closing.

Veteran's Funding Fee Chart

DOWN PAYMENT	IST TIME USE	REPEAT
0 - <5%	2.15%	3.30%
5 - <10%	1.50%	1.50%
10% or more	1.25%	1.25%
● Cash-Out Refinance	N/A	3.30%
● Rate Reduction Refinance	N/A	0.50%
● Loan Assumption	0.50%	0.50%

National Guard / Reservist Funding Fee Chart

DOWN PAYMENT	1ST TIME USE	REPEAT
0 - <5%	2.40%	3.30%
5 - <10%	1.75%	1.75%
10%	1.50%	1.50%
● Cash-Out Refinance	N/A	3.30%
● Rate Reduction Refinance	N/A	0.50%
● Loan Assumption	0.50%	0.50%

CREDIT ALERT SYSTEM (CAIVRS):

What is CAIVRS? CAIVRS is a system that shows if a person has ever defaulted on a government loan, it could be from a student loan, or an FHA or VA home loan. If a default shows up, the veteran will not be able to get a CAIVRS number and any government loan would be denied.

FHA started to use the CAIVRS system about 15 years ago. The program was successful and VA decided to join FHA in utilizing the system a few years later.

Once a veteran applies for a VA loan, the loan processor will enter the veteran's Social Security number into the CAIVRS system. The system should issue a number for the loan file. If there is an outstanding delinquent government loan, the system will not issue a CAIVRS number until the delinquent government loan is paid in full. A veteran must have a clear CAIVRS number for VA loan approval.

If a VA loan is denied, it could qualify for the VA loan appeal process. That means the lender would send the denied loan (at your request) directly to VA to appeal the decision. But, if you have a CAIVRS default, the loan denial is final until the debt is satisfied.

Occupancy Requirement:

A veteran must occupy the subject property as his or her own principal residence within a reasonable amount of time after the closing of the loan. In most cases "reasonable" means within 60 days of the closing date of the loan. Under special circumstances, a longer period of time may be considered, such as for a job transfer.

Active Duty Veteran:

Active duty military personnel may meet the occupancy requirement even if assigned overseas or other remote duty station, provided the following statement is signed by the spouse:

"My spouse is on active duty and in his/her absence I will occupy or intend to occupy the property securing this loan as my home within a reasonable period of time."

Veterans who will be released from active duty within 12 months will need to provide certain additional information. The loan package in this case must include the following for loan approval:

- A document signed by the veteran, stating that he or she has extended or re-enlisted for active duty to a date beyond the 12-month period following the projected closing of the loan.

Or

- A signed statement from the veteran that the veteran intends to re-enlist, or extend active duty to a date beyond the 12-month period following the projected closing date.

And

- A statement from the veteran's commanding officer confirming that the veteran is eligible to re-enlist or extend active duty, and the commanding officer has no reason to believe that this request would not be granted.

Or

- A valid offer of local civilian employment following release from active duty.

CHAPTER 12

VA TERMS AND GUIDELINES

- **APPRAISAL (CRV):** VA appraisals are called a Certificate of Reasonable Value.

- **ASSUMPTION:** VA loans are fully assumable with credit qualifying. A buyer does not need to be a veteran to assume a VA loan.

- **CERTIFICATE OF ELIGIBILITY:** This form indicates a veteran is eligible for a VA loan and states the amount of "Entitlement" available to the veteran.

- **CO-BORROWER:** A co-borrower, other than a spouse or same sex partner, is not eligible for a VA loan unless both the borrower and the co-borrower are veterans.

- **ELIGIBLE PROPERTY:** Eligible property for a VA loan includes a single family home, 2 to 4 unit property, a condo or a PUD that is approved by VA or FHA, and a manufactured home on its own lot, not in a mobile home park, and the manufactured home must display HUD'S certificate of conformity.

- **FEE APPRAISER:** VA maintains a list of fee appraisers, referred to as the VA Fee Panel. They are selected on a rotating basis when an appraisal is ordered from a VA approved lender.

- **FUNDING FEE:** Unless a veteran is exempt, VA charges a funding fee on all loans. If the veteran is in possession of a "VA Disability Compensation Awards Letter" this fee will be waived. This is a one time fee for each transaction and may be paid by the buyer or the seller. The funding fee may be paid in cash or financed in the loan amount. A funding fee exceeding the maximum VA loan amount must be paid in cash.

- **LAPP APPROVED:** LAPP stands for Lender Appraisal Processing Procedure. This is a designation VA gives to an underwriter after completing the training to underwrite a VA appraisal report. If the lender does not have a LAPP approved underwriter, the appraisal will be sent to VA to be underwritten, a process that can take up to 30 days.

- **LOAN ORIGINATION FEE:** This is a one time fee charged by the lender for the origination of the loan. For VA, this fee is limited to 1% of the total loan amount. Lenders charge this fee to off set the charges a VA buyer cannot pay due to VA guidelines.

- **LOAN TO VALUE:** The relationship of the VA loan to value is 100% since VA does not require a down payment. The loan amount, excluding the funding fee, would give you your loan to value .

- **MASTER CERTIFICATE OF REASONABLE VALUE:** A Master CRV is used in a new subdivision to identify all the lots in the subdivision on a VA appraisal report. As of May 22, 2009, Master CRV's will no longer be issued due to the declining market. VA will honor all existing MCRV's until their expiration date. When market conditions stabilize, VA may reinstate the MCRV.

- **MAXIMUM LOAN AMOUNT:** VA has a set loan amount throughout the country, except for high cost areas. In high cost areas the loan amount can be higher. The maximum VA limit is $417,000.00, inclusive of the funding fee. Check with your local VA office for any changes. VA Website: www.homeloans.vagov/eligibility.htm

- **MINIMUM DOWN PAYMENT:** No down payment is required if the veteran has full entitlement. A down payment of 5% or more will qualify the veteran for a lower funding fee. If the veteran has less than full entitlement, a down payment may be required.

- **OCCUPANCY REQUIREMENT:** The property must be occupied by the veteran, or the veteran's spouse, if the veteran is an in-service veteran or on active duty.

- **INTEREST RATE REDUCTION REFINANCE LOAN (IRRRL):** Refinance to a lower interest rate with no income or credit documentation. The loan program does not require an appraisal in most areas.

- **RATIO:** VA uses one ratio for qualifying the VA buyer. The guideline ratio is a 41% total debt ratio, which includes total housing expense and credit obligations.

- **RESIDUAL INCOME:** This is the balance left for family support after the total housing and credit obligations are met, including maintenance and utilities.

- **SALES CONCESSIONS:** VA limits the seller to give 4% of the appraised value as a sales concession to the buyer. If the concession is more than 4%, the loan amount must be reduced (for loan purposes only) by the dollar amount that exceeds 4%.

Example:

Sales Price $150,000 and the seller is contributing $4,000 for closing costs and $3,500 in decorating allowance. Allowable sales concession is $6,000. On this transaction, the buyer will need to come to closing with $1,500 for the overage in the allowed sales concession.

- **SECONDARY FINANCING:** A second lien is allowed with certain requirements. The interest rate on the second mortgage cannot exceed the interest rate on the first mortgage, and the second mortgage must have a term of at least five years.

- **SUBSTITUTION OF ELIGIBILITY:** This occurs when a purchasing veteran uses his or her own VA eligibility to assume another veterans VA loan in the purchase of a home. This frees up the sellers eligibility and allows the buyer to purchase the home without the expense of a new loan.

Qualifying The VA Loan:

VA uses a different approach in qualifying a borrower's credit worthiness. You will notice that VA guidelines vary in several areas from Conventional and FHA financing. Listed in the income and credit section are some of the differences from traditional financing.

One main difference is that, a borrower must have sufficient residual income left for family support after the total debt ratio is determined. Maintenance and utilities are not included in the ratios, but they are included to meet the residual requirement, based on a VA maintenance and utilities chart. Another difference is that VA qualifies a borrower on net income, not gross income. As per VA guidelines, the taxes will be taken off the borrower's monthly gross income. The underwriter can use the IRS tax charts, since the tax charts are usually less than what appears on the actual paycheck stubs.

Total Debt Ratio 41%: VA uses just one debt to income ratio for qualifying purposes, with 41% the total debt ratio guideline. This ratio consists of principal, interest, property tax, homeowners insurance, flood insurance and HOA dues, if applicable. The debt from the credit report, including any child support or alimony and child care expenses for children under twelve is also included in the ratio. Keep in mind that the ratio is only a guideline and can be exceeded with good compensating factors.

Qualifying Income:

Generally speaking, two years of employment is required for a home loan and preferably they should be in the same line of work. There are exceptions, of course, such as a young college graduate, or a veteran returning home from military duty. Here is a list of other sources of income that might be used as qualifying income.

- **Military Income** – Military quarters allowance can be used as stable income, but the veteran will need to provide a written authorization from his commanding officer for off-base housing. Flight pay, hazard pay, overseas or combat pay and miscellaneous allowances which are subject to periodic review can only be used as income if such income continued for a long period of time and is expected to continue.

- **National Guard or Reserves Income** – This type of military income can only be used if a veteran has a 24-month history, and the income will continue for three years. Otherwise it can be used to offset an installment debt.

- **Part-Time or Second Job** – A 24-month history is needed for this type of income to be considered as income. If you have a 12 to 23-month history of working part-time or a second job, the income can be used as a compensating factor or to offset installment debt.

- **Overtime and Bonus** – Again, a 24-month history of receiving this type of income is needed to be considered stable income.

- **Commission Income** – Commission income is considered as self employment. A two-year history is required as well as tax returns for the two most current years.

- **Pension Income** – Pensions can be used as income if you can provide the award letter for the pension and the pension will continue at least three years.

- **Alimony or Child Support** – Child support or alimony can be used as income as long as it will continue for three years or the child reaches 18 years of age. A copy of the final divorce decree signed by the judge is required. You will also need to provide 12 cancelled checks or bank statements as evidence of receipt of the child support or alimony with no lapse in payments.

- **Non-Taxable Income** – This includes Social Security income, disability income and Military allowances. The amount of tax savings may be added on to a borrower's income. This is called "grossing up". A figure of 15% is used to gross up and be added to the borrower's net income.

  Example:
  Social Security per month $1,200 X 15% = $180. Qualifying Income $1,380.

- **Trust Income** – Income from a trust is acceptable if constant payments are guaranteed and continue for at least three years. A copy of the trust will be needed and the trust must be irrevocable.

- **Automobile Allowance** – An auto allowance can be used to offset a car payment by determining the amount the payments exceeding the expenditures. Two years tax returns with tax Form 2106 are required.

- **Income from Room and Board** – Rental income from "Boarders" is acceptable when a relative is the boarder. The boarder's income must be reflected on the borrower's tax returns to be used as qualifying income.

- **Rental Income** – If rental income is derived from other rental property, two years of tax returns will be required along with Schedule E of your 1040's.

- **Multi-Unit Subject Property** – If the veteran intends to occupy one unit of a multi-unit property and rent out the other units, the veteran must have previous experience as a landlord to count the rental income in qualifying for the loan. The appraisers projected monthly rents will be reduced by a 25% vacancy factor. The veteran must have six months of cash reserves principal, interest, taxes and insurance (PITI), which can be verified at closing.

- **Projected Income** – Typically projected or hypothetical income is not acceptable. Exceptions are permitted under certain circumstances, such as a school teacher with a contract to start a new job when school starts in the fall, or a physician beginning a residency scheduled to start after the loan has closed. Borrowers starting a new job must present a non revocable contract for the new job and must start the new job within 60 days of the closing of the loan.

- **Changing of a Job** – It is not unusual for some borrowers to change jobs frequently. The borrower may simply be going where the work is. A borrower who has shown stabile and continuing income over a two-year period, even if the borrower has worked for a variety of employers, will be favorably considered from the standpoint of employment.

Debt From Credit Report:

Installment debt on a VA loan with ten or more payments remaining must be counted in the ratio. Any installment debt with less than ten months remaining does not have to be counted in the ratio, unless the payment is high enough to cause payment shock with a new house payment.

VA does permit "washing a payment" with income that cannot be used for qualifying the veteran. We touched on this in the income section. Let's say you have been in the military reserves for 15-months with pay of $300 per month. You would not have enough time in the military to use your reservist income to qualify. On the other hand, your auto loan is $278 per month, and the underwriter will not have to count the auto loan in the ratio because the underwriter did not consider your $300 income to qualify your loan. This is called "washing the payment."

Credit — Good or Bad

The Veterans Administration in the past has been tougher on credit standards than the FHA. It seems VA is softening a bit, and now has a new program for veterans who have been hit with the sub-prime problem we have experienced. As long as derogatory credit can be documented and the loan file reflects good reason beyond the veteran's control, VA is all for the veterans. Remember, if your loan gets denied you still have the right to appeal and have the loan package sent directly to VA for loan approval.

Collections and Judgements – Judgements must be paid off prior to the closing of your loan. Collections are on a case by case basis and need not be paid off as a condition of the loan.

Bankruptcy:

Chapter 7 – A Chapter 7 bankruptcy is one where the person who files for the bankruptcy, walks away from all their debt. To qualify for a VA home loan after a Chapter 7, the bankruptcy must have been discharged by the courts 24-months, and no exceptions. A discharged bankruptcy less than 24 months would not qualify for a VA loan approval.

Chapter 13 – This type of filing indicates an effort to pay creditors, with regular payments made to a court appointed trustee over a period of time. If the applicant has satisfactorily made at least 12 monthly payments, and the trustee, or the judge approves the new credit, it would be permissible to obtain a new home loan. Chapter 13 bankruptcy is really a re-organization, and those who file a Chapter 13 should be commended for paying off their obligation.

Foreclosure:

If a borrower had a VA or FHA foreclosure, this in itself would not disqualify the borrower from obtaining a new VA loan. However, guaranty entitlement cannot be restored unless the government's loss has been repaid in full. The veteran can ask VA to be released from the liability if the cause of the foreclosure was no fault of the veteran.

List Of VA Compensating Factors:

Every borrower should be judged on an individual basis. Here is a list of compensating factors an underwriter might use to justify a decision for approving a higher total debt ratio:

- Excellent long-term credit.

- Conservative use of credit.

- Minimum consumer debt.

- Substantial liquid assets.

- Long-term employment.

- Little or no increase in shelter expense.

- High residual income.

- Tax credit for child care.

- Tax benefits for home ownership.

- Military benefits not considered in the ratio.

- Large down payment.

- Overtime or second job income not considered in the ratio.

The list could go on, but this provides an idea of compensating factors. The total debt ratio is only a guideline and not a rule. The loan has to make sense, and if it makes sense the loan usually can be approved. The list does not apply to the residual income, the balance left for family support. If the residual income is short, the loan is denied.

VA CHILD CARE CERTIFICATION:

VA requires a complete child care statement for children under 12 years old of working parents. The cost for child care is used in the total debt ratio. If you have no cost, and a family member cares for your child, have that party complete the form.

As employed parents of minor children, I / we certify that the following information is true and correct concerning child care expenses.

My / Our children are cared for by: _____

_____

_____

_____

Whose address is: _____

_____

Telephone: _____

The cost of this care is $ _____ per week _____ month _____

_____   _____

_____   _____
           SIGNATURE   DATE

WARNING: Section 1010 of Title 18 U.S.C. Federal Housing Administration and VA Transactions, states "Whoever, for the purpose of influencing in any way the action of such Administration... makes, passes or publishes any statement, knowing the same to be false, shall be fined not more than $5,000.00 or imprisoned not more than two years or both."

Maintenance and Utilities Chart:

Maintenance and utilities will be included in the figures to determine if a borrower is over-extending himself or herself. The maintenance and utilities fees are not considered in the ratio, but they are considered in the residual, which is the money left for family support each month. The underwriter will have maintenance and utilities charts for different zones of the country, due to climate changes and other factors. The figures exhibited here are average figures and not actual figures. The utilities fees for a home in the Sun Belt areas, for example are .14 cents per square foot of the home. The costs shown below may be reduced if the property is "Energy Efficient", because solar heat was added to the home.

UTILITIES: Add-On's Per Month.

- House -   1200 square foot   x $0.14 = $ 168.00

MAINTENANCE:

- In Ground Pool $ 75.00

- Hot Tub $ 35.00

- Above ground pool $ 35.00

- Multi- Units $ 45.00 ***

_____

*** For each unit not occupied by the veteran.

What Is Residual Income?

Residual Income is the remaining income left for family support after all expenses are paid out of your total monthly income. The expenses include:

1. Total Housing Debt = Principal, interest, taxes and insurance (PITI) and homeowner association dues. (if applicable).

2. Maintenance and Utilities from the VA chart.

3. Installment Debt.

4. Revolving Charges.

5. Child Support and /or Alimony.

6. Child Care Expense.

Your loan processor will use the VA chart for the area where you live. The size of your family is also taken into consideration. The chart will show the balance VA requires for monthly living in relation to the total debt.

You can always exceed ratios with good compensating factors, but you can never be low on residual income as outlined by VA. If your residual is under what the chart states you need, your loan will be denied. The best thing to do at that point, is to see if you have an installment loan that you can pay off. That would raise your residual and give you more disposable income per month.

VA Residual Requirements:

Table of Residual Income by Region

For Loan Amounts of $80,000 and Above

Family Size	Northeast	Midwest	South	West
1	$450	$441	$441	$491
2	$755	$738	$738	$823
3	$909	$889	$889	$990
4	$1,025	$1,003	$1,003	$1,117
5	$1,062	$1,039	$1,039	$1,158

Note: Over 5 add $80 for each family member up to a family of 7.

For Loan Amounts of $79,999 and Below

Family Size	Northeast	Midwest	South	West
1	$390	$382	$382	$425
2	$654	$641	$641	$713
3	$788	$772	$772	$859
4	$888	$868	$868	$967
5	$921	$902	$902	$1,004

Note: Over 5 add $75 for each family member up to a family of 7.

VA Sales Concessions

Does your purchase contract state clearly who is paying the closing cost?

Since VA will not permit the veteran to pay a tax service fee, an underwriting fee or a fee for preparing the documents, does the contract specifically state that the seller will pay for these fees? Actually, VA does not prohibit these fees. It simply states that the lender may not charge more than 1% of the loan amount for all fees, including an origination fee. The 1% loan origination fee is meant to cover the fees the veteran cannot pay.

Sellers are permitted by VA to pay all of the veteran's closing costs and normal discount points. However, VA limits the seller to contribute no more than 4% of the appraised value as a total sales concession. If the sales concessions are more than 4% of the appraised value, then the loan amount must be reduced dollar for dollar, but that does not mean the sales price is reduced.

It is very common for a veteran to ask the seller to pay for all of the closing costs, recurring and non-recurring. This is called a **VA "No-No".** The buyer on a VA "No-No" loan would only need to come to closing with $1.00. VA requires the buyer to have something in the property, even if it is only one dollar.

When presenting such an offer, it is usually a good idea to offer the seller a purchase price closer to the asking price of the property in order to get your offer accepted, since you are asking the seller to pay all your closing costs.

What Is A Sales Concession?

Sales Concessions Include The Following:

- VA funding fee.

- Prepays (per diem interest), property tax and homeowner's property insurance.

- Discount Points to buy-down the rate, exceeding 2 points would be a sales concession.

- Furniture, patio furniture, television, pool table, etc.

- Payoffs of credit balances on behalf of the buyer.

Does the sales contract include personal property items, such as a washer and dryer, a refrigerator, or a riding a lawn mower for example? These items may or may not be considered a sales concession in your area. Each VA regional office has a list of personal property items that are acceptable as part of the sales price. If the items are not acceptable, they will be considered a sales concession. You need to contact your local VA office or visit the web for information about your area. Your local real estate agent may be able to advise on what is customary for your area as far as sales concessions are concerned.

Veterans Allowable Closing Cost

Purchase Transaction

- ✓ LOAN ORIGINATION FEE (1% of loan amount)

- ✓ LOAN DISCOUNT POINTS (up to 2 discount points)

- ✓ VA FUNDING FEE

- ✓ CREDIT REPORT ($50 - $65)

- ✓ TITLE INSURANCE

- ✓ APPRAISAL FEE ($400 - $450)

- ✓ RECORDING FEE

Refinance Transaction

The veteran will be responsible for paying the following closing costs in addition to the above closing costs connected with a purchase transaction.

- ● RECONVEYANCE FEE

- ● TERMITE INSPECTION FEE

- ● TERMITE WORK REQUIREMENTS

Veterans Non-Allowable Closing Cost

- TAX SERVICE CONTRACT

- ESCROW OR SUB ESCROW FEE

- NOTARY FEE

- WAREHOUSE FEE

- TITLE ENDORSEMENTS

- LENDER INSPECTION FEE.

- PHOTO FEE

- DISCLOSURE FEE

- HOMEOWNERS ASSOCIATION TRANSFER FEE

- DOCUMENT FEE

- DRAWING FEE

- CITY INSPECTION FEE

- SURVEY FEE

- TERMITE INSPECTION FEE (refinance only)

- TERMITE WORK REQUIREMENTS (refinance only)

- ASSIGNMENT FEE

- CITY/COUNTY TRANSACTION TAX

- LOAN PROCESSING FEE

- UNDERWRITING FEE

- ROOF INSPECTION

- COURIER FEES

- HOME WARRANTY PROGRAM

HOME LOAN GUARANTY SERVICES

Regional Loan Centers

Regional Loan Center	Jurisdiction	Mailing and Website Addresses	Telephone Number
Atlanta	Georgia North Carolina South Carolina Tennessee	Department of Veterans Affairs VA Regional Loan Center 1700 Clairmont Rd. Decatur, GA 30033-4032 (Mail: P.O. Box 100023, Decatur, GA 30031-7023) http://www.vba.va.gov /ro/atlanta/rlc/index.htm	1-888-768-2132
Cleveland	Delaware Indiana Michigan New Jersey Ohio Pennsylvania	Department of Veterans Affairs VA Regional Loan Center 1240 East Ninth Street Cleveland, OH 44199 http://www.vba.va.gov /ro/cleveland/index1.htm	1-800-729-5772
Denver	Alaska Colorado Idaho Montana Oregon Utah Washington Wyoming	Department of Veterans Affairs VA Regional Loan Center 155 Van Gordon Street Lakewood, CO 80228 (Mail: Box 25126, Denver, CO 80225) http://www.vba.va.gov/ro/denver /loan/lgy.htm	1-888-349-7541
Honolulu	Hawaii Guam American Samoa Commonwealth of the Northern Marianas	Department of Veterans Affairs VA Regional Office Loan Guaranty Division (26) 459 Patterson Rd. Honolulu, HI 96819 *Although not an RLC, this office is a fully functioning Loan Guaranty operation for Hawaii.	1-808-433-0481
Houston	Arkansas Louisiana Oklahoma Texas	Department of Veterans Affairs VA Regional Loan Center 6900 Almeda Road Houston, TX 77030-4200 http://www.vba.va.gov /ro/houston/lgy/home.html	1-888-232-2571

Manchester	Connecticut Massachusetts Maine New Hampshire New York Rhode Island Vermont	Department of Veterans Affairs VA Regional Loan Center 275 Chestnut Street Manchester, NH 03101 http://ww.vba.va.gov /ro/manchester/lgymain /loans.html	1-800-827-6311 1-800-827-0336
Phoenix	Arizona California New Mexico Nevada	Department of Veterans Affairs VA Regional Loan Center 3333 N. Central Avenue Phoenix, AZ 85012-2402 http://www.vba.va.gov /ro/phoenixlgy/	1-888-869-0194
Roanoke	District of Columbia Kentucky Maryland Virginia West Virginia	Department of Veterans Affairs VA Regional Loan Center 210 Franklin Road, SW Roanoke, VA 24011 http://www.vba.va.gov /ro/roanoke/rlc	1-800-933-5499
St. Paul	Illinois Iowa Kansas Minnesota Missouri Nebraska North Dakota South Dakota Wisconsin	Department of Veterans Affairs VA Regional Loan Center 1 Federal Drive, Ft. Snelling St. Paul, MN 55111-4050 http://www.vba.va.gov/ro/central /stpau/pages/homeloans.html	1-800-827-0611
St. Petersburg	Alabama Florida Mississippi Puerto Rico U.S. Virgin Islands	Department of Veterans Affairs VA Regional Loan Center 9500 Bay Pines Blvd. St. Petersburg, FL 33708 (Mail: P.O. Box 1437, St. Petersburg, FL 33731) http://www.vba.va.gov/ro/south /spete/rlc/index.htm	1-888-611-5916 (out of state) 1-800-827-1000 (in FL)
Winston/Salem		Department of Veterans Affairs Winston-Salem Eligibility Center P.O. Box 20729 Winston-Salem, NC 27120	1-888-244-6711

CHAPTER 13

VA REFINANCE

Cash Out Refinance: Maximum Loan Amount $417,000.00

The property being refinanced must be secured with an existing first lien in the veteran's name. This means a veteran who owns a home "free and clear" cannot obtain a VA refinance. The lien on the property can be VA, FHA, conventional financing or from a private mortgage. It would make no sense to do a VA rate and term refinance with a VA loan on the property, because that kind of loan would be refinanced under the Interest Rate Reduction Refinance program.

The loan amount that is allowed for a VA refinance is based on two formulas related to the loan to value ratio. VA will allow 90% of the appraised value or 75% of the appraised value plus $36,000, the lessor of the two.

For example, let us say the appraised value of the property is $275,000.

FORMULA #1 – 90% of $275,000 = $247,500

FORMULA #2 – 75% of $275,000 = $206,250+$36,000 = $242,250 (New Loan)

FORMULA #2 was the lessor amount of the two examples in this case.

The dwelling must be the veteran's primary residence and be occupied by the veteran. The only exception is if the veteran is on active duty. Occupancy by the spouse is sufficient to meet the occupancy requirement. An appraisal from an approved VA appraiser and a credit package is required.

Veterans with Sub-Prime Loans:

Veterans with sub-prime conventional home loans now have new options for refinancing through the department of Veterans affairs. A law was signed October 28 2008 allowing the following changes due to the sub-prime mortgage fiasco. These changes will allow VA to assist a substantial number of veterans that have sub-prime mortgages. Under the new law, veterans who wish to refinance their sub-prime conventional mortgage may now do so for up to 100 percent of the appraised value.

Additionally, Congress raised VA's maximum loan amount for these types of refinancing loans. Previously, refinance loans were capped at $144,000 except for the interest rate reduction refinance loan. With the new legislation, such loans may be made up to $729,750 depending on where the property is located.

Interest Rate Reduction Refinance Loan (IRRRL):

One of the best features of a VA loan is being able to refinance to a lower interest rate with no credit qualifying and no out of pocket expense, and you won't even need an appraisal in most cases. The veteran must be in good standing with the lender and the loan must be current over the last 12-months. Also, the veteran must own the property that is being refinanced with the following exceptions:

- The veteran whose entitlement was used to purchase the home has died, and the veteran's unmarried surviving spouse was obligated on the existing loan and still owns the property.

- The existing loan was assumed by a veteran who substituted his or her entitlement.

The interest rate on the new loan must be lower than the interest rate on the old loan. There is an exception if the veteran is refinancing from an adjustable rate mortgage to a fixed rate mortgage, or from a 30-year loan to a 15-year loan. In this situation, the payment on the new loan cannot increase more than $50.00 per month or the veteran will need to credit qualify.

Cash out refinance is not allowed in this program. If necessary the new loan amount will be rounded down to avoid any cash going back to the veteran.

The term of the new loan cannot exceed the term of the existing loan by more than 10 years, with a maximum term of 30 years, whichever is less.

Refinancing Your Rental Property

A veteran who does not currently reside in a home where he once lived and which he still owns, can also use the IRRRL program. The veteran must provide evidence for the loan file that he once lived in the property, and is now renting out the home. In this case he can take advantage of the lower interest rate without qualifying for the loan and not be charged high refinance fees.

Loan Fees For an IRRRL:

- ✓ 1% Loan Origination Fee

- ✓ 0.50% Funding Fee

- ✓ Title Insurance

- ✓ Reconveyance Fee

- ✓ Recording Fee

An appraisal is not listed here because it is not required in most areas of the country. VA does permit a veteran to pay reasonable discount points to buy an interest rate down. Go to the conventional section to read if paying discount points is right for you.

NOTES

CHAPTER 14

LOAN ASSUMPTION

What is a Loan Assumption? Loan assumptions should be used more. A legal loan assumption occurs when a buyer takes over a seller's existing assumable mortgage note. This practice is not only legal, but also preferred because it will save the buyer thousands of dollars in closing costs for not originating a new loan. The buyer must qualify for the loan through the lender who holds the mortgage note.

Back in 1978 to 1982, interest rates went from 10.0% to 17.0%. Because interest rates were so high, everyone was assuming the existing loan on a property, and that was the only way the property could be sold. Banks and Savings and Loans put a stop to assuming fixed rate conventional loans because they were losing revenue, and a-la, the ARM loan was born. Since 1983, all fixed rate conventional loans are not assumable, but ARM loans are assumable, as well as FHA and VA loans.

What Is A Non-Assumable Loan? Fixed rate conventional loans are no longer assumable, but there are ways around this, by handling your transaction in the form of a "Land Contract" or a "Wrap Around". You would not go through the lender to qualify for the assumption, the seller will decide if he would like to sell you his home in that fashion. Payment will be made each month directly to the seller or a non-interested third party, such as an escrow office.

How to Assume an Existing Mortgage Lien:

Assuming an existing mortgage loan is really the way to go for your home financing for many reasons. Loan assumption is not to be shied away from, it is just another avenue to purchase property that many people forget about.

In a market such as we are experiencing in 2008 - 2009, when money is tight, loan assumption is really a great option for home financing. It can be a win-win for the buyer and the seller, especially if the seller does not have an immediate need all his money out of the sale of his home, and he can afford to carry a mortgage for the buyer in a second lien.

When you find a property to purchase, ask the seller or the real estate agent what kind of loan is on the property and if the loan is assumable. If you find the loan is assumable, you will need to know the interest rate and the remaining term of the loan to know if it is acceptable to you. Before making any decisions, ask to read the Note and the Deed to the property, along with any addendums recorded with the Deed.

What Loans are Assumable?

Most ARM loans are assumable, but they have shorter term or balloon payments. All government loans such as FHA and VA is assumable. The only loan that is not assumable at the present time is a conventional fixed rate loan, but that loan can also be assumed if the seller is willing to sell his home to you on a Land Contract or a Wrap around. A Land Contract is like a wrap around, the payments are made directly to the seller or a non interested third party.

Example of a Land Contract or a Wrap Around:

Let us say the buyer and the seller agreed on a sales price of $250,000 for the sellers home. The buyer is making a 10% down payment of $25,000. The existing conventional mortgage balance on the home is $185,000 @ 5.5% interest. The seller agrees to carry a second mortgage of $40,000 @ 7.50 interest, with interest only payments on the 2nd lien for five years with a balloon payment at maturity (in five years).

The payments for the Ist and 2nd mortgages would be sent directly to the seller. The seller would take his payment for the 2nd mortgage $250.00, and send the balance to the original lender. I realize there would need to be trust on both ends. One might have a comfort level with having a non interested third party handle the monthly payments, of course there would be a monthly fee for the service.

This procedure would not have to occur if the seller's loan is assumable. In that case the buyer or the seller would call the lender of record, give the loan number and ask to have an assumption package forwarded to you or the seller. The lender would handle your paper work, as far as changing names on the lien.

With any assumption contract, and especially, anytime a seller is carrying a lien on the property you are purchasing, hire a real estate attorney to read the purchase contract. The attorney will give you sound advice and draw up the second mortgage for you. It will be well worth the several hundred dollars in attorney fees for the piece of mind and know your contract is written for your protection.

Example of a VA loan assumption

VA loans are assumable to anyone. Contrary to what people think, you do not need to be a veteran to assume a VA loan. If you assume a VA loan the seller's VA eligibility will be tied up until you pay off the loan. If the buyer is a veteran, so much the better because the veteran purchasing the property can use his or her own VA eligibility and the seller's VA eligibility will be restored at closing. This is called a "Substitution of Eligibility."

You will save thousands of dollars in lender's fees by assuming an existing loan rather than originating a new loan. Lenders may vary by a few dollars in assumption fees, but only on their fees for the credit report and the flood certification. The fees stated below are from a major bank.

Assumption Fees of a VA Loan.

VA Funding Fee on loan assumptions is 0.50% of the loan balance.

- 1% of the unpaid principal balance with a cap of $500.00

- Credit Profile   14.00

- Flood Certification   8.00

- VA Funding Fee 0.50% of the loan amount?   _____

                 Total Lender Cost $522.00 + Funding Fee

Assumption Fees of a FHA Loan:

An FHA loan, like a VA loan, can be assumed by anyone, but you will need to credit qualify through the lender who is holding the mortgage. The lender's cost for an FHA loan assumption is shown below:

- 1% of the unpaid principal balance with a cap of $500.00

- Credit Profile 14.00

- Flood Certification 8.00

- Total Lender Assumption Cost $522.00

Assumption Fees of a Conventional Loan.

- 1% of the unpaid principal balance with a cap of $900.00

- Credit Profile $14.00

- Flood Certification $8.00

- Total Lender Assumption Cost $922.00

Typical Loan Assumption Contract

Let us say you find a home you love and you make an offer to purchase the property. The first existing mortgage on the property is FHA, so it is an assumable loan. The loan originated in 2002 with a $152,850 loan amount. The interest rate @ 5.75%, is a fixed rate for 30 years. The current outstanding loan balance is $143,250 with 23 years remaining on the loan.

The seller of the property and you agree on a sales price of $189,900. With a 10% down payment from you, the seller is willing to carry a second mortgage for you. The interest rate for the 2nd mortgage is 8.00%, amortized over 15 years with a 5-year balloon payment.

The scenario will look like this:

Sales Price	$189,900.00
10% Down Payment	18,990.00
1ST Mortgage Assumed (PITI)	$143,250.00 = $1,176.00 (payment on 1st)
2ND MORTGAGE from seller	$ 27,660.00 = $ 264.33 (payment on 2nd)
Total	$189,900.00 = $1,440.33 (monthly payment)

Note: In assuming the FHA first mortgage, the payment includes principal, interest, property taxes, homeowners insurance and MMI.

Example showing contrast of cost with a new FHA loan using the same sales price.

You can see the huge savings in closing costs by assuming the previous owner's mortgage. But, if you plan to keep the home for a long time, then I would suggest you go for the new loan, simply because the assumption contract would probably have a balloon payment with the seller carrying the second mortgage. On the other hand, when the marketplace experiences declining values, you might be able to assume someone's loan without having to have a second mortgage. Then the assumption would make sense and you would save thousands of dollars in closing costs and lender's fees. Example of originating a new FHA loan:

Sales price	$189,900.00	
Down pay	- 6,646.50	3.5% Down Payment
	$183,253.50	Loan amount without up-front MIP
Add up-front MIP +	3,206.93 =	.93 cents must be pain in cash

Total loan	$186,459.50 (@ 5.75%) = $1,088.12 (P&I)	
	tax & Insurance, monthly	285.00
	MMI, paid monthly	100.79
	Total Monthly Payment	$1,473.91 PITI

The closing costs and the lender's fees for this example, would be approximately $5,600.00 and that is a very conservative figure. Add another $3,000 or more, for pre-pays, depending on the time of year your loan closes. Pre-pays are taxes, insurance and per diem interest. You will not have this extra expense with a loan assumption.

CHAPTER 15

SUBORDINATE FINANCING

There are different types of subordinate financing. A subordinate loan is a junior loan under your first mortgage. An Equity Line of Credit is a junior loan, a second or third mortgage is also a junior loan. I mentioned a third mortgage, this type of loan is more prevalent in a hot real estate market. Listed below are the more common types of second liens.

EQUITY LINE OF CREDIT - An equity line of credit is credit given on your property based on the total loan to value including the line of credit, this is called CLTV. You will be given a check book for an agreed amount of money. You can pull funds from that line of credit at will. Your payment is based on the amount of money you have spent, not the maximum amount on the line of credit. The conclusive loan to value varies with lender to lender, it pays to shop.

SECOND MORTGAGE - A second mortgage has set monthly payments. The loan can be amortized over 15-years or maybe 15-years with a balloon. A second mortgage can also be originated when the property is purchased. Many lenders offer a loan called 80/10/10. What that means is, with a 10% down payment, the lender is financing your first mortgage with a 80% loan. The lender will carry a 10% second mortgage for you so you can avoid paying private mortgage insurance. Many people also take out a second mortgage for home improvement.

Seller Carry Back Second Mortgage

Mortgage Notes can vary on interest rates and terms of the loan. Typically, a seller-carried second mortgage, will have an interest rate 2.0% to 3.0% higher than the going rate in the market place of a first mortgage. If the going rate at the time of purchase for a 30-year fixed rate note is 6.0%, the seller would charge 8.0% to 9.0% interest to carry your note. A seller would probably ask for higher interest for a buyer with negative credit.

What is the reason for the higher rate? That answer is the risk factor. The higher the risk, the higher the rate and vice versa.

Here are three examples of a seller carry-back second mortgage note.

- Amortized over 15 years with a five year Balloon.

- Interest only payments all due in five years.

- Straight Note all due in five years with no payments.

This is just an example of how you can structure a mortgage with the seller. You can take any of these mortgages and change the term with a balloon payment.

Whatever the buyer and seller agree upon would constitute a contract. If the seller is taking back a second mortgage for you, I suggest you have a real estate attorney look over your purchase contract, it will be well worth the attorney's fee.

Discounted Mortgage Note

If your private second mortgage note was designed with a balloon payment in five, seven or ten years, you could ask the note holder to discount the note for early repayment. Many people that carry notes would love to be paid off early. You will never know unless you ask.

Wait until there are 12-24 remaining payments on the note. If you have the resources to pay off the note early, then by all means do it. Write a letter or make a phone call to the note holder and ask if he or she is willing to discount the note for early pay off. Not everyone will accept this offer. If the note holder is responsive to your offer, you can ask how much the note will be discounted or you can make the note holder an offer. The discounted rate should be anywhere between 10 and 15 percent and it is based on the unpaid balance. For example, if the note is interest only or a straight note, the discounted dollar amount could be substantial because it will be based on the entire note, nothing has been applied to principal.

Let us say you owe a $50,000 second mortgage and you have been paying interest only payments. The note has a 5-year balloon, 8.0% interest with payments of $333.33 per month.

Discounted note @ 15% = $7,500 off the face of the note = $42,500.00 Balance due.

If your second mortgage note is a 15-year amortized loan with no balloon payment, you can still ask for a discount with early repayment and you can do this anytime during the term of the loan. The problem I see here, the seller agreed to a long term note. Probably the seller did this for the investment feature so the motivation might not be there.

For The Seller's Protection

I know we talked about the buyer of a property, but now I want to talk to the seller of a property. It has been a rough real estate market the last couple of years. It will turn around, it always does. I can't think of a better opportunity to make up some of the money lost in the stock market. A seller carried back second mortgage would help get your home sold and earn you interest you could never get in a Certificate of Deposit. The going rate for a second mortgage is 2% to 3% higher than the going market rate for first mortgage loans.

There is really very little risk. If you decide to carry a second mortgage on your property, always hire a real estate attorney to go through the contract. It will be well worth his fee for the piece of mind. He can draw up the second mortgage for you and he will file a "Notice of Default" on your behalf.

The Notice of Default is your protection against the property going into default with the first lien holder. What happens if the property does enter into foreclosure? If the Notice of Default is filed, by law, the lien holder of the first lien must notify the lien holder of the second lien that the property has entered into foreclosure. This will give notice to the second lien holder, and he could redeem the property and protect his investment.

In Carrying A second Lien On Your Property

#1.) Always run a credit report on the buyer so you know the character of the person. A credit report says volumes about a person.

#2.) You must have at least six months payments on the property liquid in the bank or don't even consider carrying a second. The funds will be needed if the property enters into foreclosure so you can take back your property.

#3.) Always hire a real estate attorney. Have the attorney file a "Notice of Default."

CHAPTER 16

FORECLOSURES IN TODAY'S WORLD

Generally, there is only one method by which to force payment of a mortgagor that fails to make payment as agreed and that is to institute an action in the court called FORECLOSURE SUIT. When the court trial is held and a default is established, the court orders a sale of the property to be held by the Sheriff or Court Commissioner. The Notice of Sale must be posted in a public place for 20 days and published once a week for 20 days.

For millions of Americans, the dream of home ownership has become a nightmare because of unscrupulous loan agents and the mortgage industry in general. One would think their party is over, but agents who prey on the weak are already getting ready for round two.

I am sure you heard of the loan modification program, and companies that promise they can stop your foreclosure in its tracks. Don't you believe it! The way the scam works, the company will "guarantee" it can stop your foreclosure and help a homeowner through the loan modification process. They promise to get you a better interest rate and better terms as well. The up-front fee is from $1,000 to $3,000. After collecting the money, the company does little, if anything, to assist the homeowner. The company doesn't contact your lender and does not modify your loan in any way.

The Federal Trade Commission, along with the Department of Treasury, the Justice Department and the Department of Housing and Urban Development have joined efforts to aggressively go after mortgage modification and home foreclosure rescue companies. These operations are swindling desperate homeowners out of money they cannot afford to lose. It is very sad that the trust is lost in so many ways. I hope you report to the federal government anyone who tries to modify your mortgage loan for money. We need to get these people off the streets.

Legitimate Non-Profit Housing Counselors:

If the loan modification company is legitimate, you will never pay one cent for the help you will get from a housing counselor. You can call your local HUD office or go on line at www.hud.gov. for help. The service is free of charge and the HUD counselors work with your lender, so there is someone there to help you.

Many people at this time are losing their homes to foreclosures. Many have also lost their jobs and many were caught with a sub-prime loan. Whatever the reason, banks today need to work with people because people are hurting. Property values have declined and many people can't refinance, even though they want to. I have tried to help several of my friends refinance their homes. The lenders do not care, they take your call and put you on hold for an eternity.

I just read a story about several members of Congress who tried to help their constituents by picking up the phone themselves to negotiate with the lenders on behalf of their constituents. The pain of being put on hold for long periods of time can be an educating experience for a member of Congress. As a body, Congress has failed to come up with a broad fix for the foreclosure crises. Some lawmakers are helping homeowners one at a time and seeking creative ways to make a difference.

I don't know what it is going to take to get banks working with the public again. Banks could do more than they are doing to help people. The banks offer a 40-year mortgage and yet they charge a higher interest rate for the 40-year mortgage. Wouldn't it be better to offer a 40-year mortgage to a person about to lose their home at a reasonable interest rate? For the life of me, I don't see their logic for not wanting to do everything in their power to save a home, and not have a property back on their books. I can understand, the interest rate on a 40-year mortgage would be a few ticks above a 30-year mortgage, but the lenders are charging 2 percentage points above the 30-year mortgage. Do you see what I mean, the lenders could be doing a lot more than they are.

The time line for a foreclosure is a 90-day redemption period and 120 days to sale. What that means, the first 90 days the foreclosure notice was filed, the homeowner can redeem the property through a sale of the property, loan modification or other means. The lender takes over from 91 days through the 120 days, when the property goes to sale.

Buying a Foreclosure

In the past, buying a foreclosure was usually a pretty good deal. With the declining real estate values, that concept is no longer true. Remember, VA requires no down payment and FHA requires very little down payment. For the most part, unless you can work out forgiveness for part of the principal balance, the property is probably over encumbered. Look for properties that the loan originated at least seven years prior.

Most foreclosures are bought **AS IS**, usually they do not allow for a home inspection, you must use caution when buying a foreclosure. Don't get me wrong, there are still good buys to be had in foreclosures, but it will take a lot of research. Just the other day I heard that someone snapped up a foreclosure in Ponte Vedra, Florida, one block from the ocean for $95,000. Ponta Vedra is very upscale, this is an unheard of price for that area.

If you want to investigate the foreclosure market, I would suggest signing up for a realty service company that tracks foreclosures such as Realty Trac. These companies usually give you a free trial period and if you join after the trial period, the price is very reasonable for what they do. They will alert you of properties in foreclosure in the zip code in which you are interested. A lot of the leg work is done for you.

Short Sales are also a great avenue to getting a good price on a property. You will need patience, because a short sale can take forever to purchase. You submit your offer and then the bank has to decide if they want to take your offer, they move at a snails pace.

With so many people not being able to sell their homes in today's market, foreclosures and short sales might not be the best option. Many people are very motivated to sell their homes and you would not be dealing with distressed properties. I don't understand for the life of me why more loan assumptions are not taking place in this market.

With all the distressed properties in the marketplace, I have read articles where some of the appraisers are using foreclosures as their comparables in appraising a property. This is unfortunate, and it is so unfair to the buyer and the seller, this practice will only decline our market further. Sure, from time to time an appraiser will need to include a foreclosure when other properties are not available. When that occurs, the appraiser should add a forth comparable even if it is further away, and adjust heavily for the use of the foreclosure, because it is a distress sale.

Good-Buy My Friend

If I have left you with anything in writing this book, I would want have instilled the most important aspect of buying a home: **NEVER BUY MORE HOUSE THAN YOU CAN AFFORD.** Most people buy a home on emotion, and that is easy to do, but remember, you need to be responsible for the payments.

I sincerely hope I have given you something of value, my mission is to give you the tools needed to navigate through the mortgage loan application process. I know it can be a daunting task.

We have gone through conventional loan financing as well as FHA and VA loan programs. I hope you read all three sections to determine the best financing for yourself. You have the tools to know the difference between Reasonable Closing Cost and Unreasonable Closing Cost. To know when to pay Discount Points and when you are wasting your money. Watch Rebate Pricing to be sure you are getting the Rebate. After reading this book you might want to consider assuming a loan, you will save thousands of dollars in closing cost in doing so.

I wish there was a litmus test to weed out the loan SHARKS from the good loan agents, but there is not. It will be up to you to read the red flags brought up in the book.

Because of the complexity of the mortgage banking industry, I cannot be responsible for guideline changes. From time to time with the economic conditions, maximum loan amounts, income documentation and the loan to value limits will change. The premise of loan financing will remain the same and that is why this book will never become outdated. It will be your responsibility to find the current maximum loan limits and loan to value guidelines during the time period you are buying a home.

I know I will have my critics in writing this book, I knew that going in. If I was afraid what my colleagues would say this book would have never been written. I hope I have just as many supporters from the mortgage banking industry.

INDEX

INDEX

Amortization	7, 18
Amortization Chart	34
Appraisal	18, 115
Arm Loans	29, 80
Assumption Loan	18, 76, 129, 156
Authorized Signer	50
Balloon Loan	29
Banks	9
Bankruptcy	49, 94, 138
Buyers Market	24
Buy-Down Financing	31
Certification of Occupancy	18
Chattel Mortgage	18
Collections	48, 94, 137
Condominium	18, 27, 42, 80
Conventional Loan Programs	28
Credit History	48, 94, 137
Credit Report	15
Discount Points	36
Discounted Mortgage Note	165
Escrow Account	18
Equity Line of Credit	163

FICO Scoring		12
Foreclosure		49, 94, 138, 167, 169
Funds to Close Loan		55, 99
Federal Housing Administration		65, 76
FHA	2-4 Units	32, 100
FHA	Arm Loan	80
FHA	Assumption	76, 160
FHA	Cash on Hand	99
FHA	Closing Cost	84
FHA	Condo Guidelines	80
FHA	Credit Guidelines	93
FHA	Energy Efficient	103
FHA	Funds to Close Loan	99
FHA	Gift Funds and Gift Letter	99
FHA	Income Guidelines	95
FHA	Kiddie Condo	77
FHA	Loan Limits	69
FHA	Loan Origination Fee	77
FHA	Loan Programs	80
FHA	Maximum Loan	70, 77
FHA	Minimum Down Payment	70, 77
FHA	Mortgage Insurance Premium - MIP	71,. 78
FHA	Mutual Mortgage Insurance - MMI	72, 78
FHA	Ratio Guidelines	93
FHA	Refinance Programs	105
FHA	Refinance - Cash out	107
FHA	Refinance - Streamline Refinance	108
FHA	Rent Credit	99
FHA	Sales Concessions	74

FHA Secondary Residence	79	
FHA Up-Front MIP	71	
FHA Up-Front MIP Refund	73	
Gift Letter	55, 99	
Good Faith Estimate	9, 77	
Graduated Payment Loan (GPM)	31, 80	
Home Inspection	26	
Homeowners Insurance	19	
Housing Counselors	168	
Impound Account	18	
Index	19, 82	
Interest Only Loan	32	
Judgement	48, 94, 137	
Land Contract	158	
LendingTree.com	11	
Liabilities	46, 97, 137	
Life Cap	30, 82	
Loan Application (1003)	39	
Loan Lock	38	
Loan Origination Fee	77, 130	
Loan to Value - LTV	19, 39, 77, 130	
Margin	19, 82	
Mortgage	19	
Mortgage Broker	9	

Mortgage Insurance Premium - MIP	71, 78
Mutual Mortgage Insurance - MMI	72, 78
Negative Amortization Loan	31
No Doc Loan	32
Non Purchasing Spouse	98
Non Recurring Closing Cost	6
Notice of Default	166
Par Pricing	35
Planned Unit Development - PUD	19, 27
Pre-Approval	17
Premium Pricing	35
Pre-Payment Penalty	33, 78
Private Mortgage Insurance - PMI	20, 41
Purchase Contract	21, 25
Qualify the Conventional Loan	44
Qualify the FHA Loan	93
Qualify the VA Loan	133
Rate Sheet	35
Ratio's	45, 78, 133
Rebate Pricing	35
Recurring Closing Cost	6
Red Lining	2
Reduced Doc Loan	32
Refinance the Conventional Loan	57
Refinance with Cash Out	60
Refinance with a Junior Loan	61

Sales Concessions   74, 79, 132, 144

Second Mortgage   79, 163

Seller Carry Back Financing   164

Sellers Market   24

Sellers Protection   166

Single Family Residence   20, 43

Subordinate Financing   163

Trust Deed   20

Units   20, 27, 100, 129, 141

Veterans Administration - VA   113

VA Active Service Veteran   127

VA Appraisal   129

VA Assumption   129

VA Certificate of Eligibility   118, 129

VA Child Care Statement   140

VA Closing Cost   146

VA Credit Guidelines   137

VA Down Payment   117

VA Entitlement   119

VA Fee Appraiser   129

VA Funding Fee   124, 130

VA Funding Fee Chart   125

VA History of VA Entitlement   120

VA LAPP Approved   130

VA Loan Amount   117

VA Loan Limits   116

VA Loan Origination Fee   130

VA Maintance and Utilities   141

VA Master Certificate of Reasonable Value   130

VA Maximum Loan Amount   131

VA Minimum Down Payment   131

VA Non Allowable Closing Cost   147

VA Occupancy Requirements   127, 131

VA Qualify the VA Loan   116, 133

VA Qualifying Income   134

VA Ratio   131, 133

VA Refinance   150

VA Refinance - Cash Out   150

VA Refinance - Interest Rate Reduction   152

VA Refinance - Rental Property   153

VA Regional Offices   148

VA Residual Chart   143

VA Residual Income   131, 142

VA Restoration of Entitlement   123

VA Sales Concession   132, 144

VA Secondary Financing   117, 132

VA Substitution of Eligibility   132

Veterans with Sub-Prime Loans   151

Wrap Around Mortgage   158